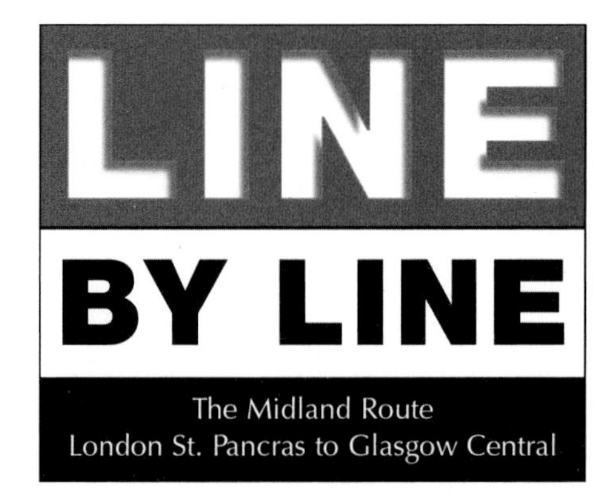

MARTIN BUCK

&

MARK RAWLINSON

Freightmaster
Publishing

CONTENTS

Schematic Maps & Research : Mark Rawlinson
e-mail : mark.rawlinson@virgin.net
fax : 01524-730591

Layout, Text & Captions : Martin Buck
e-mail : martin.buck@btconnect.com
fax : 01793-644079

ISBN : 0-9537540-3-0

Published by : Freightmaster Publishing
158 Overbrook
SWINDON
SN3 6AY

Printed by : Stephens & George, Mertyhr Tydfil

Front Cover Designed by : Artworking Ltd, Purton

INTRODUCTION

THANK YOU for buying this copy of LINE BY LINE, the fourth book in our series of fully illustrated guides on famous railway routes.

THIS EDITION covers the old 'Midland Route' from London St. Pancras to Glasgow Central which, unlike previous routes in this series, calls into play some artistic license so as to follow the course of this famous route as closely as possible.

The original route between Sheffield and Leeds went via Cudworth but, as this section of track has long been lifted, we have routed our journey via Moorthorpe, Hare Park Junction, Normanton and Woodlesford. Furthermore, as it is difficult to show reversals schematically, both Nottingham and Leeds City stations have been excluded.

By taking this action, a continuous journey has been preserved throughout.

EVERY PAGE you turn will reveal a ten-mile, schematic, cross section of the route spread across two pages showing a gradient profile & topography, track plan and station layouts along with two recent photographs to illustrate locations of interest.

Periodically, this sequence is broken with several pages of more than one photograph to illustrate additional locations. The photographs also provide representative coverage of both the motive power and rolling stock associated with the Midland Route around the turn of the second Millennium.

We start at St. Pancras station, from where the route is traced northward in 5-mile sections until our journey is completed over 400 miles later.

A 'GALLERY' section features a selection of high calibre colour photographs to illustrate some classic locations on the Midland Route, notably where the route is blessed with magnificent scenery - the 'Settle & Carlisle' line over the Pennines along with the former Glasgow & South Western Railway where the route courses the River Nith. Full-colour reproductions of Ordnance Survey Landranger maps are also included to show the location of each view.

FINALLY our thanks go to the Ordnance Survey for allowing us to reproduce their Landranger maps and those people named overleaf, who have kindly contributed photographs for inclusion in this volume.

We also extend our thanks to those of you who have purchased this and the other three volumes of Line By Line; we hope they have brought you interest and enjoyment in our coverage of railway routes out of London.

ACKNOWLEDGEMENTS

Ordnance Survey

The map extracts in the 'Gallery' are included to help pinpoint locations. They are kindly reproduced from the following Landranger 1 : 50 000 scale Ordnance Survey maps by permission of Ordnance Survey on behalf of the Controller of Her Majesty's Stationary Office, © Crown Copyright MC0100028152:

Sheet	Landranger Map	Date	'Gallery' Photographs
71	Lanark & Upper Nithsdale	2002	1 to 4
78	Nithsdale & Annandale	2002	5 to 10
91	Appleby-in-Westmorland	2003	11 to 13
98	Wensleydale & Upper Wharfedale	2002	14 to 22
103	Blackburn, Burnley, Clitheroe & Skipton	2003	23 & 24

Photographs

The people who have kindly contributed material for this book are named below along with a note of their initials, which have been used throughout for the purpose of accreditation.

Robert Armitstead	(RA)	Bob Avery	(BA)	Chris Booth	(CB)
Martin Buck	(MB)	Phil Chilton	(PC)	Nigel Gibbs	(NG)
Dave McAlone	(DM)	Brian Morrison	(BM)	Gavin Morrison	(GM)
Robin Ralston	(RR)	Peter J Robinson	(PJR)	John Whiteley	(JW)

Brief details of the non-captioned photographs are as follows:

Page	Location	Description	By
11	Wellingborough	47488 : 1B19, Nottingham - St. Pancras	MB (04/02)
81	Arten Gill	66044 : 6U51, Ayr - Drax	MB (03/02)
97	Kirkconnel	156503 : 1M82, Glasgow - Carlisle	DM (04/00)
123	Ratcliffe-on-Soar	HST : 1B43, Nottingham - St. Pancras	MB (04/03)

Bibliography

Railway Track Diagrams (1. Scotland)	: Quail Map Company	ISBN 1-898319-51-0
Railway Track Diagrams (2. England : East)	: Quail Map Company	ISBN 1-898319-29-14
Railway Track Diagrams (4. England : Midlands)	: Quail Map Company	ISBN 1-898319-29-4
Rail Atlas (GB & Ireland)	: Haynes Publishing	ISBN 0-86093-534-5
Gradient Profiles	: Ian Allan Ltd	ISBN 0-7110-0875-2
Freightmaster*	: Freightmaster Publishing	ISSN 1357-4841
Class One*	: Freightmaster Publishing	ISSN 1465-6973

* various editions used for train identification purposes.

OVERVIEW

Background:

When travelling from London to Scotland, one is inclined to think of only two routes, the West Coast route from Euston and the East Coast route from King's Cross. But, for many years, there was a third and that was the Midland Route.

This route ran out of St. Pancras up the spine of England to Glasgow and, although not the quickest route to Scotland, provided an important direct Anglo-Scottish service for towns and cities in the East Midlands and South Yorkshire. Indeed, the Midland Route proved popular and in its heyday leading up to the Great War, the Midland ran five daily Anglo-Scottish express services in Summer and three in Winter. Alas, in the 1980's, services stopped serving St. Pancras altogether, running between Nottingham and Glasgow instead, reduced further by the 1990's to a 'Sprinter' service between Leeds and Carlisle.

Of course, one train was synonymous with the Midland Route - the Thames Clyde Express - and we are basically retracing the route taken by this famous train from London to Glasgow.

The old Midland Route today is a piecemeal collection of lines and is definitely the poor relation when compared to its neighbours - the ECML and WCML. Modernisation has been slow and its importance has been somewhat reduced as a result of the withdrawal of through passenger services between St. Pancras and Glasgow.

However, the route still provides a valuable function today. On the southern section, having secured the franchise following the privatisation of British Rail, *Midland Mainline* operate inter-city passenger services out of St. Pancras to Derby, Nottingham, Sheffield and Leeds. In contrast, the northern section between Settle Junction and Glasgow is equally important, providing a diversionary route when the WCML is closed for engineering work and being a freight artery, especially for the movement of Scottish coal to English power stations.

The route is not straightforward in terms of management and operations, unlike the other three routes in this series which all have a single Train Operating Company responsible for running through passenger services. Furthermore, the route uniquely passes through three different regions of the former British Rail (Midland, Eastern and Scottish, respectively) and can be categorised into four separate, identifiable, sections, thus:

- the Midland Mainline (St. Pancras to Leeds)
- the Aire Valley (Leeds to Skipton)
- the Settle & Carlisle
- the ex-Glasgow & South Western Railway (Carlisle/Dumfries/Glasgow)

Historical Perspective :

Two years after the opening of the Liverpool & Manchester Railway, a 16-mile line was completed between Leicester and Swannington. This new line formed the nucleus of a railway system which would eventually extend to over 1,500 miles in England, 265 miles in Ireland and a further 1,354 miles of leased and joint lines, to make the Midland Railway the third largest system in the British Isles.

For a time, the Leicester & Swannington remained an isolated railway. However, during 1839/40 the Midland Counties line was being opened from Rugby to Leicester and Trent, where it branched into lines serving Derby and Nottingham. At the same time, the North Midland Railway was being completed from Derby to Leeds, as was the Birmingham & Derby line. In 1844 the railways converging on Derby joined forces to form the Midland Railway, which absorbed the Leicester & Swannington in 1845.

In the 1850s, Parliamentary powers were obtained to build a line southward from Leicester through Kettering to Bedford and thence to a junction with the Great Northern Railway over which running powers would be exercised into King's Cross - the first Midland trains made their way into London for the first time in 1858.

However, the final 32 miles from Hitchin to King's Cross proved too congested and so the Company made plans to continue the main line through St. Albans into their own terminus. In 1868, Midland trains started entering St. Pancras station, complete with Barlow's magnificent roof and Scott's opulent hotel with Gothic frontage.

Northward out of St. Pancras the route is very fast, except for slowing at Wellingborough, Market Harborough and Wigston, where the ex-Midland Counties line from Rugby trails in. Mining subsidence proved problematical in the Erewash Valley in later years and as the line pressed on to Leeds, it took advantage of low ground and bypassed such places as Sheffield and Wakefield, save for branch lines. The alignment in this area was good but, yet again, mining subsidence spoilt its quality.

The Midland Route followed the "Old Road" between Chesterfield and Rotherham, constructed by George Stephenson and opened in 1840 as part of his North Midland Railway from Derby to Leeds. The Sheffield & Rotherham Railway was opened in 1838 from Wicker station to Rotherham Westgate, with a spur at Holmes Junction to join the North Midland line at Masborough.

Sheffield became accessible from the south in 1870 when the railway was opened from Chesterfield through Dronfield to Sheffield Pond Street - Midland station as we know it today. The direct line from Chesterfield to Sheffield became the main line, (the section covered in this book) with stations on the "Old Road" closing in the 1950s and the route becoming a diversionary and 'freight only' line.

From Leeds, the route meanders up Airedale; the line to Shipley formed part of the Leeds-Bradford line built in 1846, with the Shipley-Skipton section completed in 1847. Both parts were operated by the Midland Railway until 1923 and then the LMS until the railways were nationalised in 1948.

After Skipton, the Midland worked an independent line nicknamed the 'Little' North Western to Carnforth. From Clapham Junction, the line branched off to Ingleton, where it made an end-on junction with a branch of the LNWR coming south from Low Gill, on the WCML. This route provided a service for Midland passengers to Scotland, but it proved unsatisfactory and the Company set out to have its own line from Settle Junction to Carlisle; the necessary authority being obtained in 1865.

After pressure from the two Scottish railways which were to be the Midland's partners north of the Border - the Glasgow & South Western and the North British - work on the line was eventually started in 1869. It would be built at very high cost and under great difficulty due to the terrain involving heavy tunneling and bridgework. However, the Midland was undeterred and accorded the project the utmost priority in its attempt to forge its own slice of the Anglo-Scottish market.

The line was finally opened in 1876 and the first Midland trains ran on their own metals throughout from London St. Pancras to Carlisle, thence over their partner's G&SW route to Glasgow, albeit St. Enoch terminus in those days.

The 'S. & C.' was, and still is, a remarkable railway. No less than 13 tunnels were needed and 12 major viaducts had to be built in order to keep gradients reasonably even and alignment good. Weather on the 'S. & C.' could be atrocious, with high winds whipping tarpaulins off freight wagons and heavy drifting snow, necessitating snow fences to be constructed, such as those above Dent, the remains of which are still visible today! The line, as a result, boasts some fascinating statistics:

- Ais Gill: the summit of the line at 1,167ft; over 250ft. higher than Shap.
- Ribblehead viaduct: 24 arches, 440 yards long, 100ft. high.
- Dent station: at 1,100ft. is the highest main line station in England.
- Garsdale: the site of the highest water troughs in the world.
- the project took 6 years to complete involving 6,000 workmen.
- the cost was nearly £3.5 million.

However, in spite of all the difficulties, it became a trunk route and with a time penalty of about an hour compared to the West Coast route, it became a route solely to suit Midlands passengers for Scotland. Ultimately, it was overtaken by events as the Settle & Carlisle became the railway no-one wanted and faced possible closure in the late 1980s.

Upon reaching Carlisle, the Midland Railway route met up with six other railway companies and between 1875 to 1922, each of the seven pre-1923 companies had their own locomotive shed! Leaving Carlisle, the route follows the ex-Caledonian Railway (WCML) to Gretna Junction where it leaves the main west coast route to join the ex-Glasgow & South Western Railway via Dumfries to Glasgow.

The line via Nithsdale was the inspiration of the Glasgow, Dumfries & Carlisle Railway company, who built a line between Gretna and New Cumnock to link up with an extension of the Glasgow, Kilmarnock & Ayr Railway to complete the line between Carlisle and Glasgow. The first part between Gretna Junction and Dumfries opened in 1848 and throughout on 28 October 1850, the date on which the two railway companies amalgamated to become the Glasgow & South Western railway.

Although the G&SW was an easier, if not longer, route, the line did feature engineering works greater than any on the the Caledonian route to Glasgow. For example, there is the 1,410yds. long Drumlanrig Tunnel near Carron Bridge and Ballochmyle viaduct, 10 miles south of Kilmarnock. Ballochmyle is the largest masonry arch and the highest railway bridge in Britain, with the central span over the River Ayr covering 181ft. and 169ft. above the river bed - possibly the biggest masonry span in the world!

Gradients :

From a gradient perspective, the Midland Route is more onerous than the WCML and considerably more so than the ECML.

Between St. Pancras and Leicester there is a switchback of gradients, mostly at 1 in 176 to 200 as far as Bedford, then inclines of 1 in 119 and 1 in 200 over Sharnbrook summit at 315ft. above sea level. There are further steepish climbs as far as Leicester, prior to which, the line breasts Desborough summit at 436ft.

From there, perhaps rather surprisingly, the route is relatively level until the line negotiates the Pennines. From Settle Junction, there is a gruelling 1 in 100 ascent for 15 miles to Blea Moor - affectionately, known as the "Long Drag" - in the opposite direction, a very similar climb from Appleby to Ais Gill, where the line reaches a maximum altitude of 1,167ft.

Over the border, the gradients are notable as the the line passes through scenic Nithsdale and the Drumlanrig Gorge, in particular, skirting the Lowther Hills in the process. The line reaches 616ft. at Polquhap summit and there are some stiff climbs between Kilmarnock and Glasgow, as steep as 1 in 70 before reaching Dunlop. In the opposite direction, there is another gruelling ascent of 1 in 99/100 between Kilmarnock and Mossgiel.

Modernisation & Signalling :

Progress in this field has been relatively slow and piecemeal, to the extent that even the main line between Wellingborough and Sileby was still semaphore less than 20 years ago!

As part of the 1955 Modernisation Project, St. Pancras was resignalled and a new power signalbox was commissioned in October 1957, replacing 5 conventional lever frame signalboxes in the area and was the first panel installed by the London Midland Region. In December 1969 a new powerbox was completed at Trent, which along with new ones at Saltley and Derby controlled a total of 242 route miles and ultimately replaced 180 mechanical signalboxes. Apparently, at Trent, some 8 men per shift had to deal with over 500 train movements each day!

In November 1976, the Government approved electrification of suburban services out of St. Pancras to Bedford, including a new power signalbox at West Hampstead which ultimately replaced all signalboxes between St. Pancras and Wellingborough. In July 1982, resignalling was complete and in September the same year the overhead electric lines were switched on.

It was not until June 1983 that approval was given for the resignalling of the Midland main line between West Hampstead and Trent - nicknamed, the 'Leicester Gap'. A new signalling centre was built at Leicester and by the time it was fully operational in December 1987, 22 manual boxes had been replaced. This meant that Multiple Aspect Signalling (MAS) was now operational from St. Pancras to Clay Cross Junction and thence northward to Leeds.

Between Sheffield and Skipton, the old Midland Route has seen significant change since 1980. A new station has been built at Meadowhall (linking up with the Sheffield Metro system) on the site of former steel mills to serve one of the largest retail centres in Europe; Rotherham (Masborough) station has closed, replaced by Rotherham Central on a completely different line.

Some 9 miles of track between Swinton and Cudworth has been lifted (resulting in a re-routing of services) and extensive track rationalisation has been carried out in the Normanton area with the much-photographed junction at Goose Hill being taken out altogether. Finally, in the 1990s, the Aire Valley line was fully electrified between Leeds and Skipton.

Much of the track between Hellifield and Glasgow is still as it always has been, controlled by semaphore signalling, albeit now in longer block sections as a result of signalboxes, such as Dent and Ais Gill, for example, being de-commissioned.

However, the old Midland route still has much to offer and despite there no longer being any through passenger services from which to enjoy its splendour in one go - please now do the next best thing, turn the page and retrace this historic route from the comfort of your own armchair, Line By Line!

LEGEND

An Overview

In compiling this book, the route has been split into five-mile sections, with one section per page. Each section comprises:

- A gradient profile
- A track plan
- A photograph

The Gradient Profiles

These show a 'cutaway' side-on view of the section, exaggerated enough to clearly show the changing gradients of the route. There is also a vertical scale, marked in 200 foot increments; the highest point on the route is Ais Gill Summit which is 1,167ft. above sea level.

The Track Plans

These show a 'birds eye' view of the route, with running lines, junctions, etc. clearly marked. It should be noted that these plans are schematic and, while the maps themselves are to scale, certain features have had to be slightly enlarged to maintain clarity.

Key to Symbols

To make the diagrams in the following pages easy to use, symbols and abbreviations have been kept to the absolute minimum:

(grey bar)	= station platform (in use)	*U.G.L.*	= Up Goods loop
(empty box)	= station platform (disused)	*D.G.L.*	= Down Goods Loop
SB	= signal box	*U.P.L.*	= Up Passenger Loop
PSB	= power signal box	*D.P.L.*	= Down Passenger Loop
⊠	= disused signal box	⋮	= Boundary between signal box areas
....	= trackbed		

St. Pancras to Carlisle

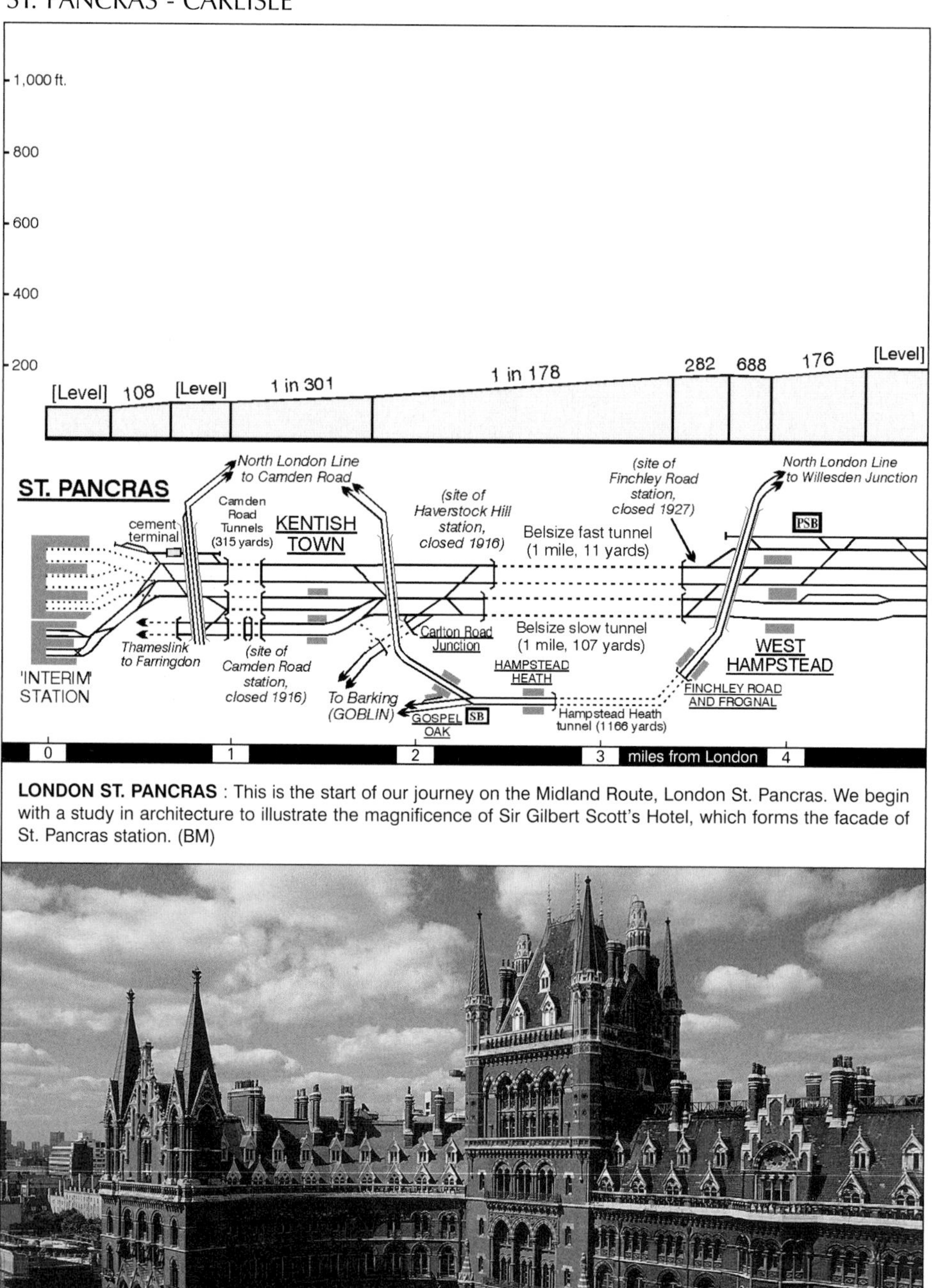

LONDON ST. PANCRAS : This is the start of our journey on the Midland Route, London St. Pancras. We begin with a study in architecture to illustrate the magnificence of Sir Gilbert Scott's Hotel, which forms the facade of St. Pancras station. (BM)

ST. PANCRAS : Looking back into the original trainshed, four Midland Mainline HSTs (*above*) await their next turn of duty, and one can see how Barlow's splendid wrought iron trainshed now looks very dated!. (BM 07/01)

During the compilation of this book, construction work began on the new *Eurostar* passenger terminal at London St. Pancras. The illustration (*below*) shows some of the work being undertaken, as viewed from an HST arriving at the London terminus, running as 1B55, the 1830 ex- Nottingham. During this period, the electrification was switched off and the "Bed-Pan" suburban electrics were diverted away from the station. (NG 07/03)

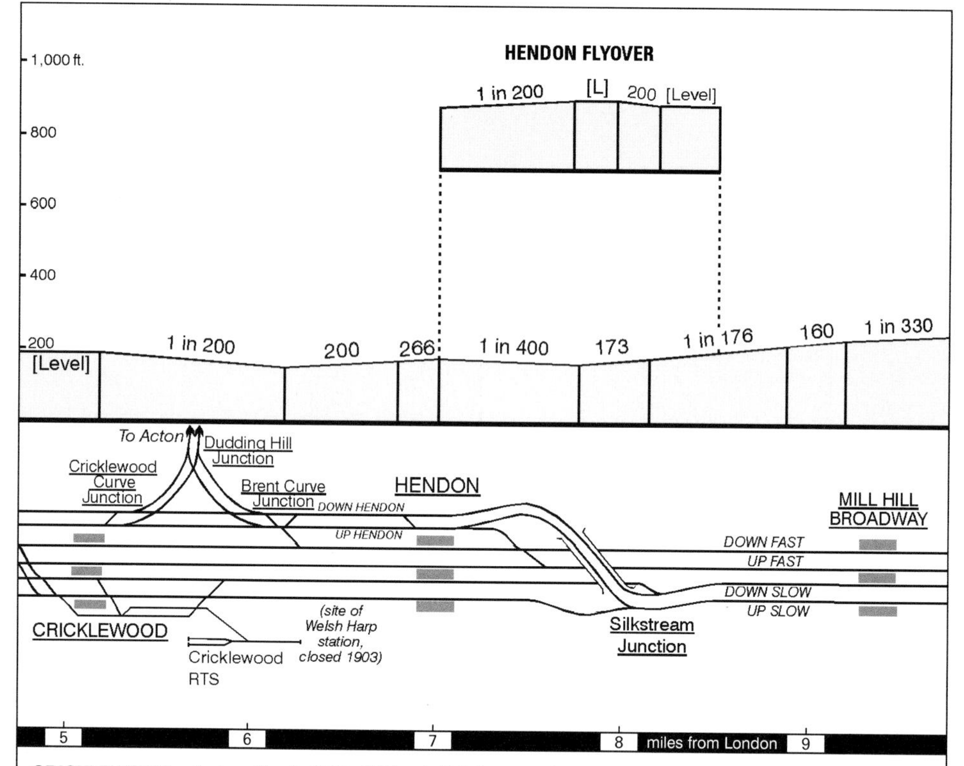

CRICKLEWOOD : During March 2003, Midland Mainline unveiled the first of it's 16-strong HST fleet to be refurbished; the overhaul of 36 class 43 power cars and re-fitting of 127 Mk. 3 carriages by Maintrain. Here, the first HST set to be completed in the new "Ocean Blue" and silver livery is entering Cricklewood, forming 1B27, the 1130 Nottingham - St. Pancras. The power cars are 43166/43074, respectively. (NG 03/03)

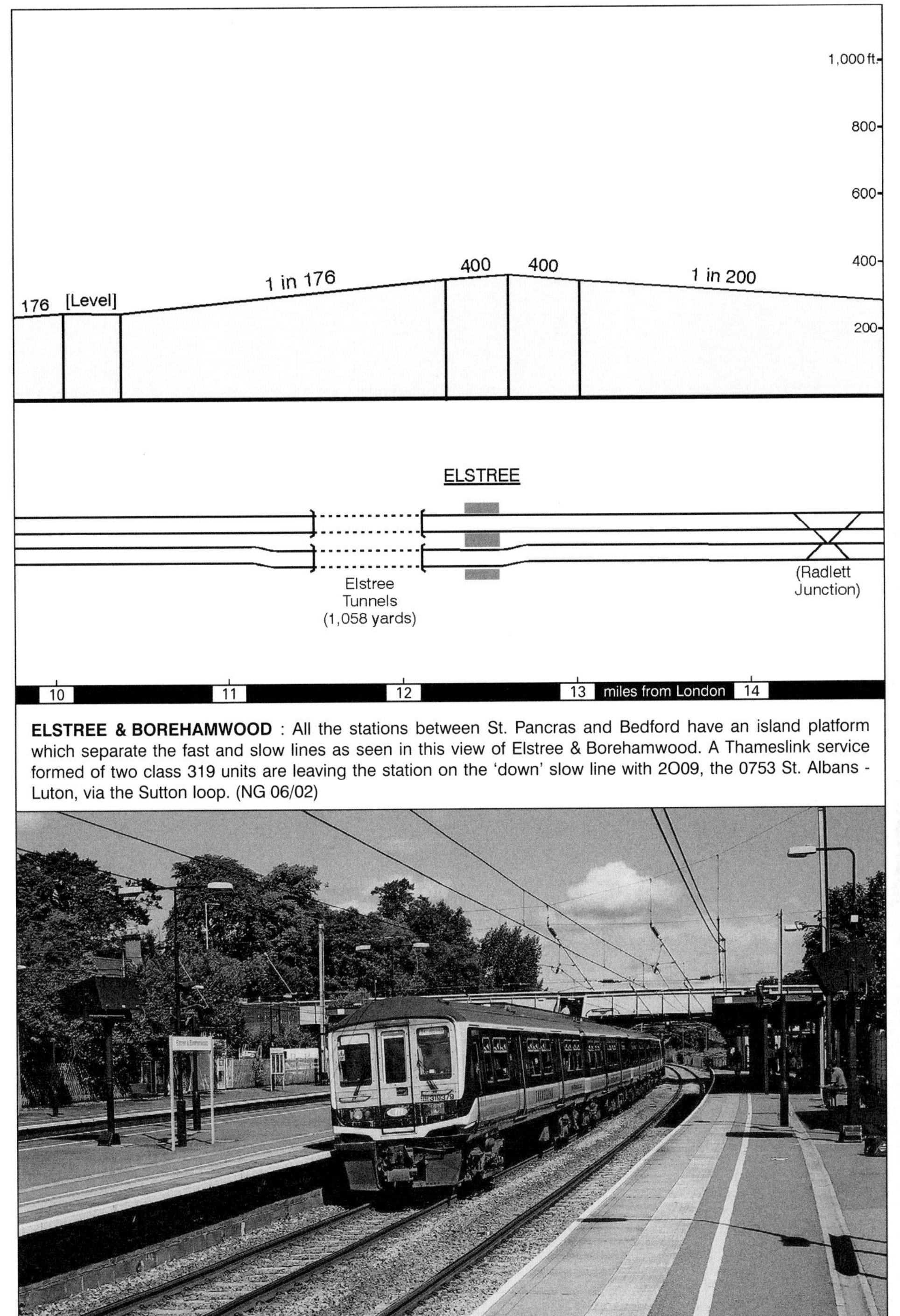

ELSTREE & BOREHAMWOOD : All the stations between St. Pancras and Bedford have an island platform which separate the fast and slow lines as seen in this view of Elstree & Borehamwood. A Thameslink service formed of two class 319 units are leaving the station on the 'down' slow line with 2O09, the 0753 St. Albans - Luton, via the Sutton loop. (NG 06/02)

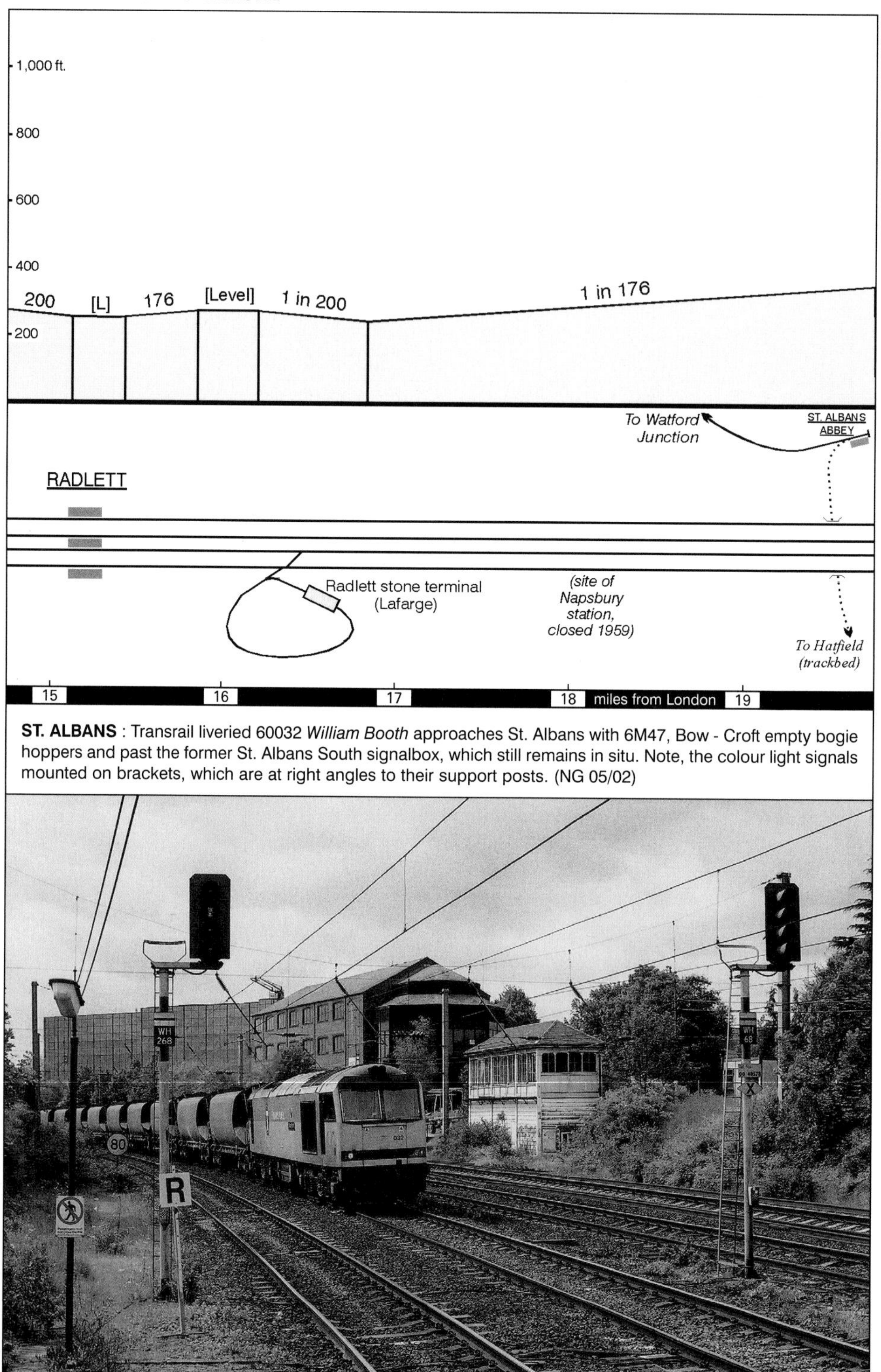

ST. ALBANS : Transrail liveried 60032 *William Booth* approaches St. Albans with 6M47, Bow - Croft empty bogie hoppers and past the former St. Albans South signalbox, which still remains in situ. Note, the colour light signals mounted on brackets, which are at right angles to their support posts. (NG 05/02)

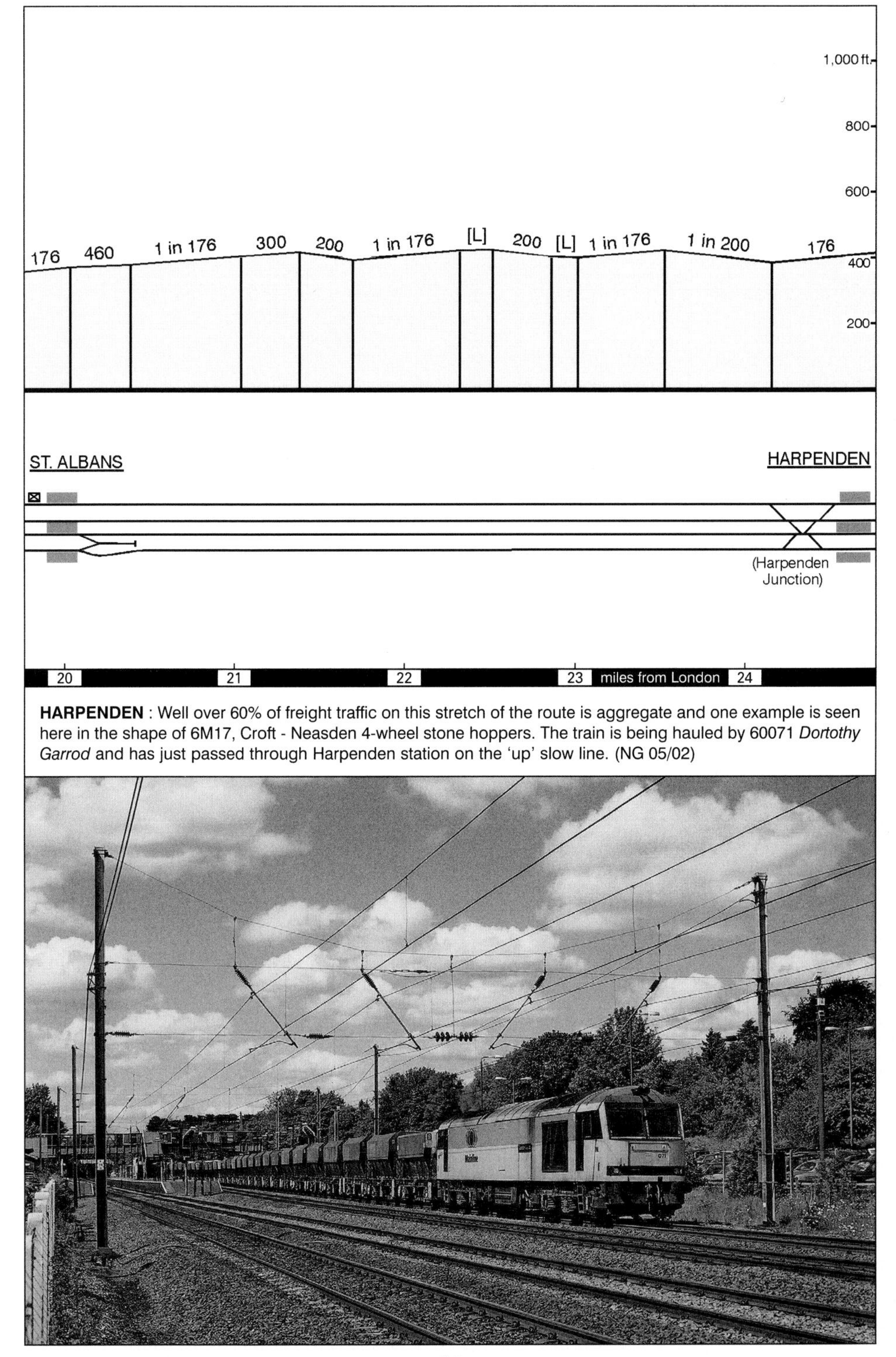

HARPENDEN : Well over 60% of freight traffic on this stretch of the route is aggregate and one example is seen here in the shape of 6M17, Croft - Neasden 4-wheel stone hoppers. The train is being hauled by 60071 *Dortothy Garrod* and has just passed through Harpenden station on the 'up' slow line. (NG 05/02)

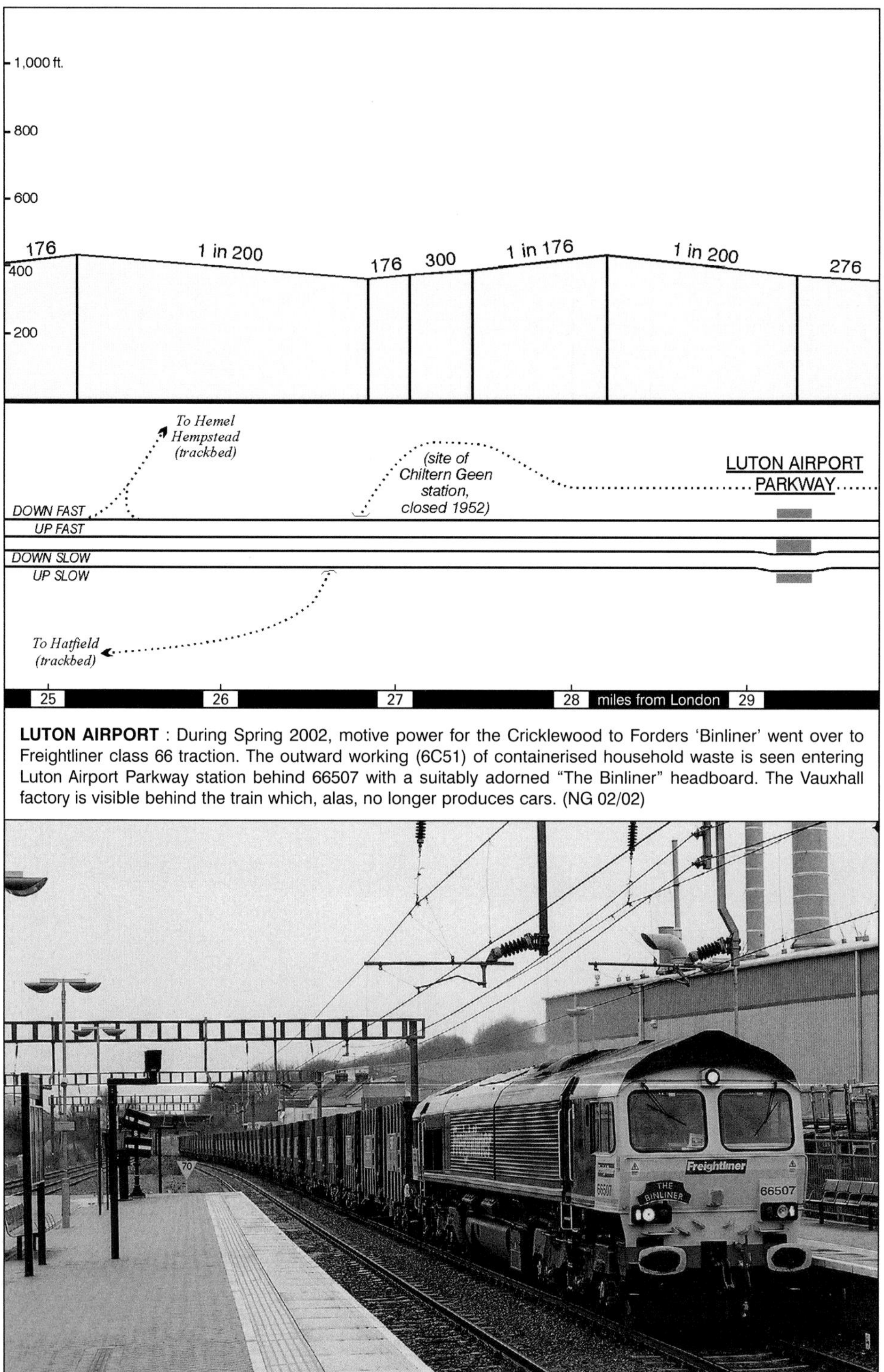

LUTON AIRPORT : During Spring 2002, motive power for the Cricklewood to Forders 'Binliner' went over to Freightliner class 66 traction. The outward working (6C51) of containerised household waste is seen entering Luton Airport Parkway station behind 66507 with a suitably adorned "The Binliner" headboard. The Vauxhall factory is visible behind the train which, alas, no longer produces cars. (NG 02/02)

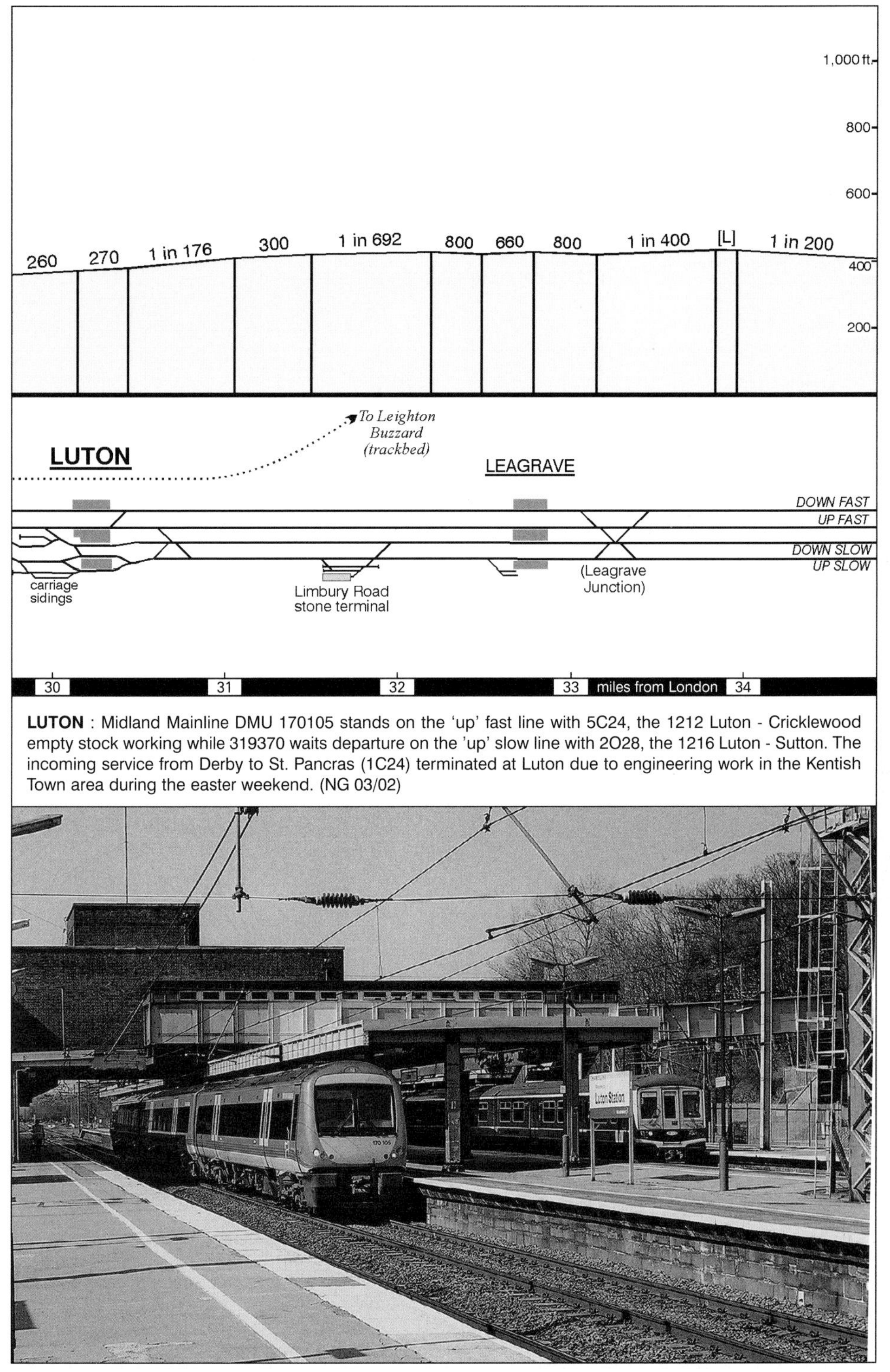

LUTON : Midland Mainline DMU 170105 stands on the 'up' fast line with 5C24, the 1212 Luton - Cricklewood empty stock working while 319370 waits departure on the 'up' slow line with 2O28, the 1216 Luton - Sutton. The incoming service from Derby to St. Pancras (1C24) terminated at Luton due to engineering work in the Kentish Town area during the easter weekend. (NG 03/02)

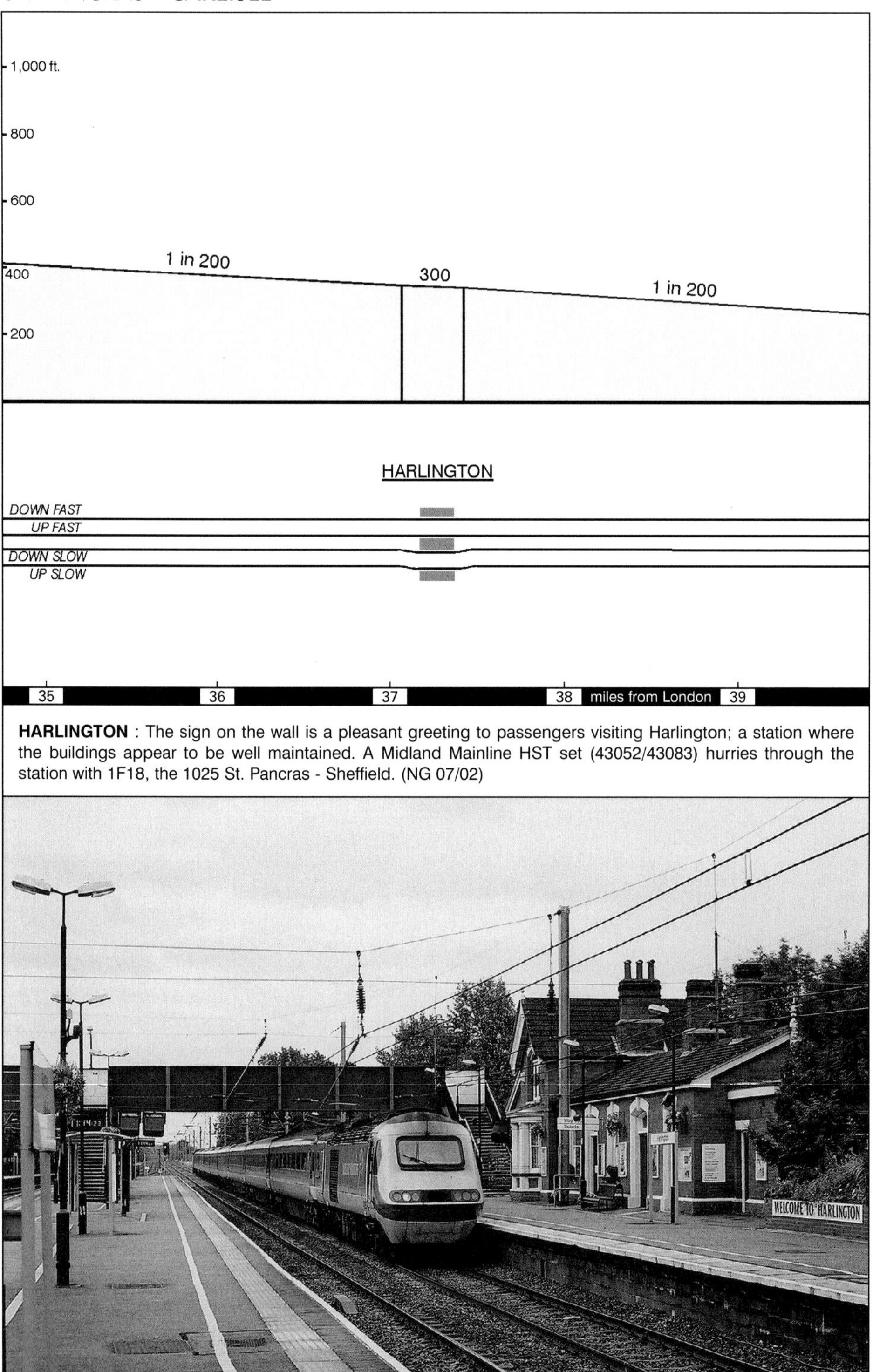

HARLINGTON : The sign on the wall is a pleasant greeting to passengers visiting Harlington; a station where the buildings appear to be well maintained. A Midland Mainline HST set (43052/43083) hurries through the station with 1F18, the 1025 St. Pancras - Sheffield. (NG 07/02)

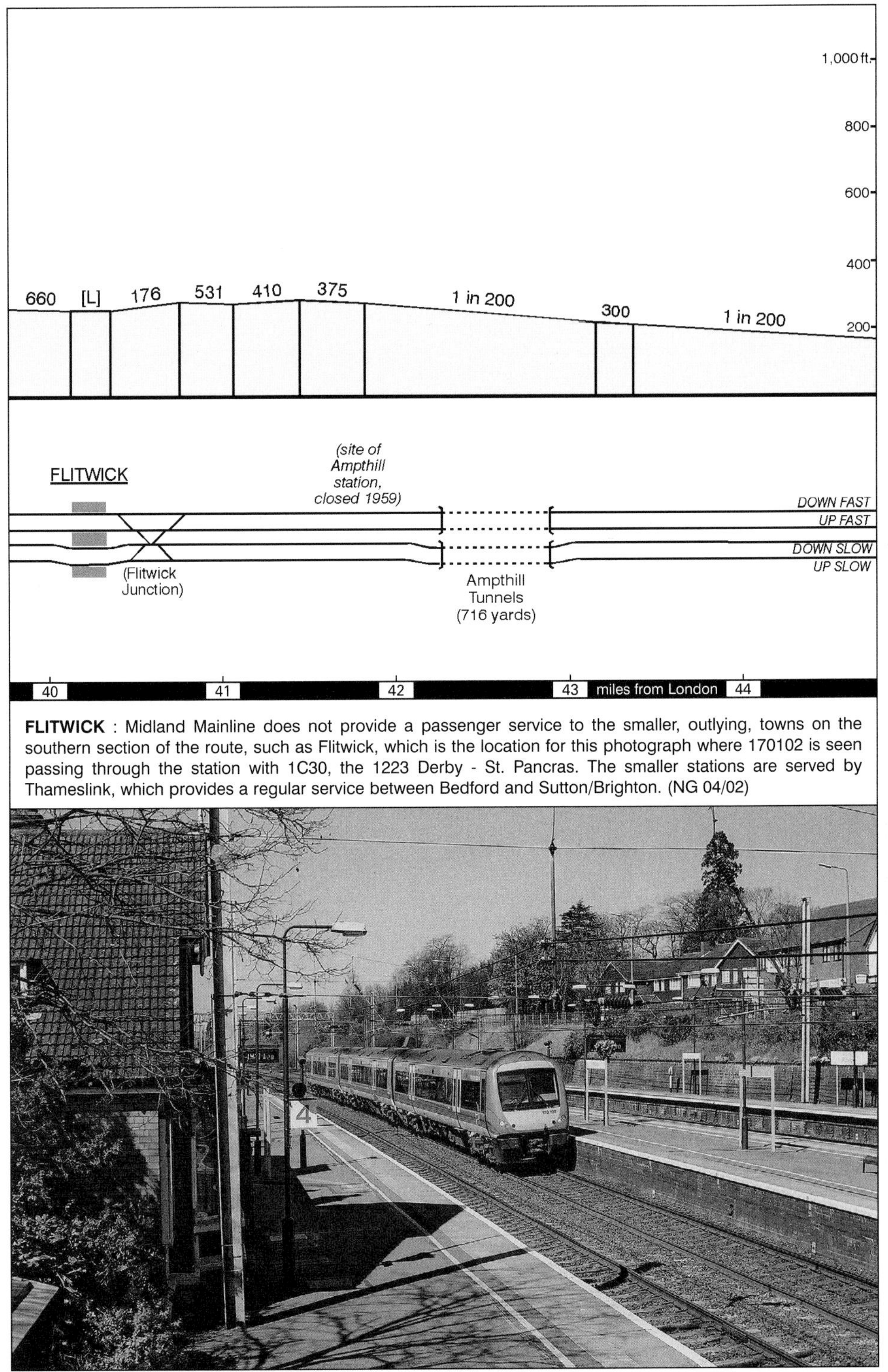

FLITWICK : Midland Mainline does not provide a passenger service to the smaller, outlying, towns on the southern section of the route, such as Flitwick, which is the location for this photograph where 170102 is seen passing through the station with 1C30, the 1223 Derby - St. Pancras. The smaller stations are served by Thameslink, which provides a regular service between Bedford and Sutton/Brighton. (NG 04/02)

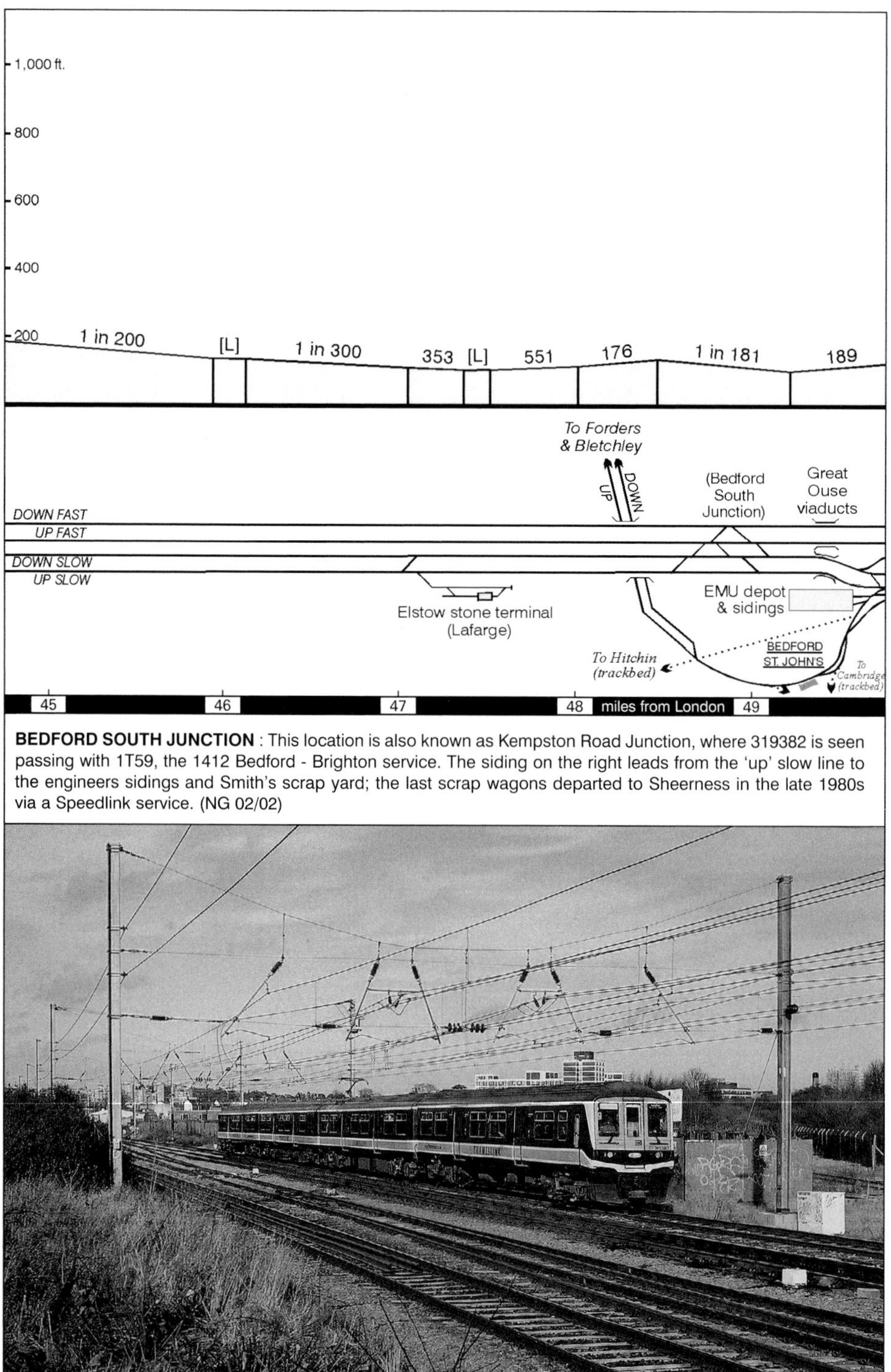

BEDFORD SOUTH JUNCTION : This location is also known as Kempston Road Junction, where 319382 is seen passing with 1T59, the 1412 Bedford - Brighton service. The siding on the right leads from the 'up' slow line to the engineers sidings and Smith's scrap yard; the last scrap wagons departed to Sheerness in the late 1980s via a Speedlink service. (NG 02/02)

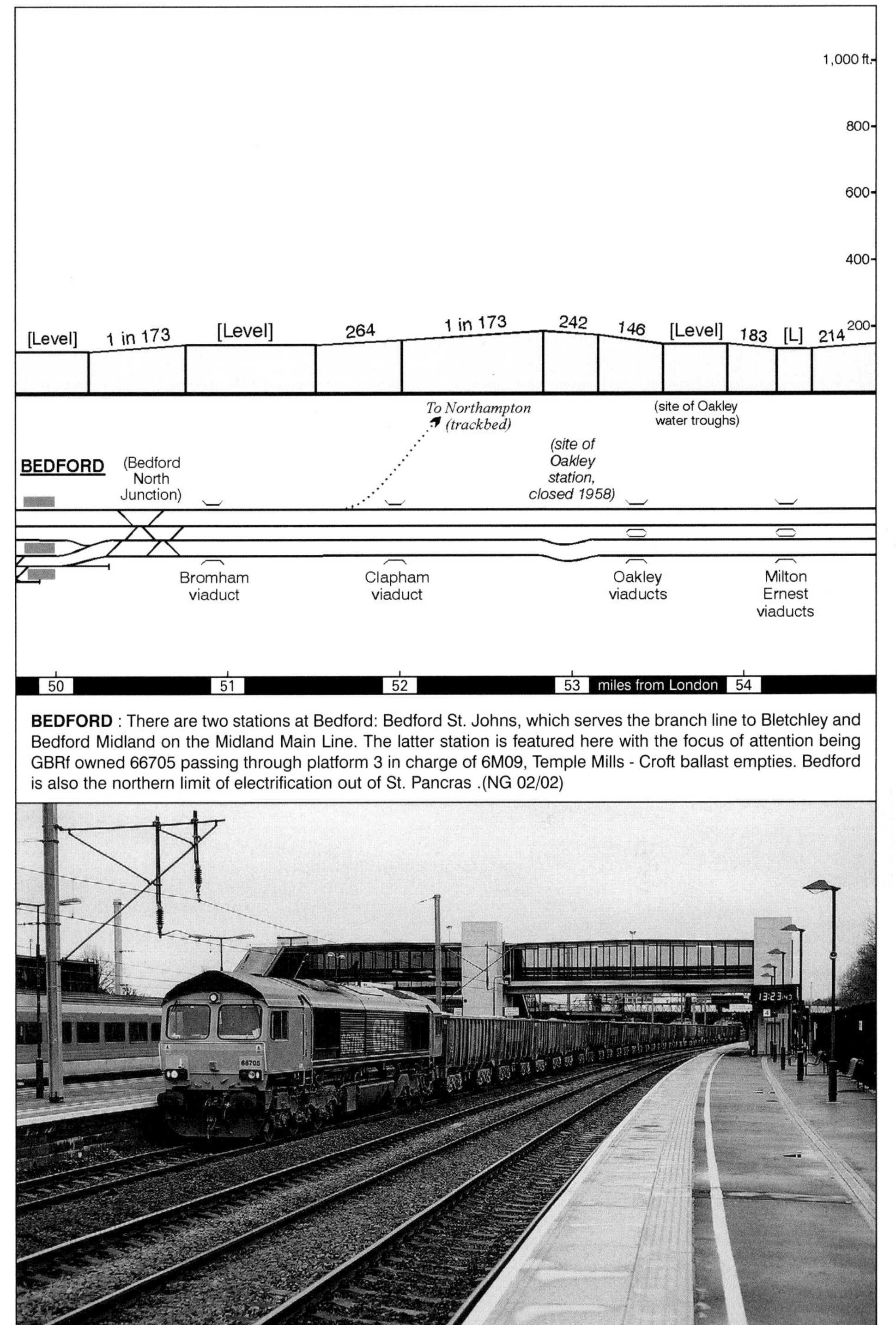

BEDFORD : There are two stations at Bedford: Bedford St. Johns, which serves the branch line to Bletchley and Bedford Midland on the Midland Main Line. The latter station is featured here with the focus of attention being GBRf owned 66705 passing through platform 3 in charge of 6M09, Temple Mills - Croft ballast empties. Bedford is also the northern limit of electrification out of St. Pancras .(NG 02/02)

WYMINGTON SLOW LINE

220
1 in 160
1 in 846

400
200
215
1 in 180
200 158 100
1 in 119

West Hampstead PSB
Leicester SC

(site of Sharnbrook station, closed 1960)

DOWN FAST
UP FAST
DOWN SLOW
UP SLOW
UP & DOWN SLOW

Radwell viaducts
Sharnbrook viaducts
(Sharnbrook Junction)
Wymington Tunnel (1 mile 90 yards)

55 56 57 58 miles from London 59

SHARNBROOK : This part of the route near the villages of Sharnbrook and Souldrop is interesting because the running lines are on different levels. The 'up' and 'down' fast lines are situated on one level whilst a bi-directional slow line passes at a lower level and through Wymington (Sharnbrook) Tunnel. This unique feature is shown to good effect here with 60092 *Reginald Munns* travelling along the slow line near Sharnbrook hauling a lengthy rake of empty bogey oil tanks forming 6E50, Langley - Lindsey. (NG 10/99)

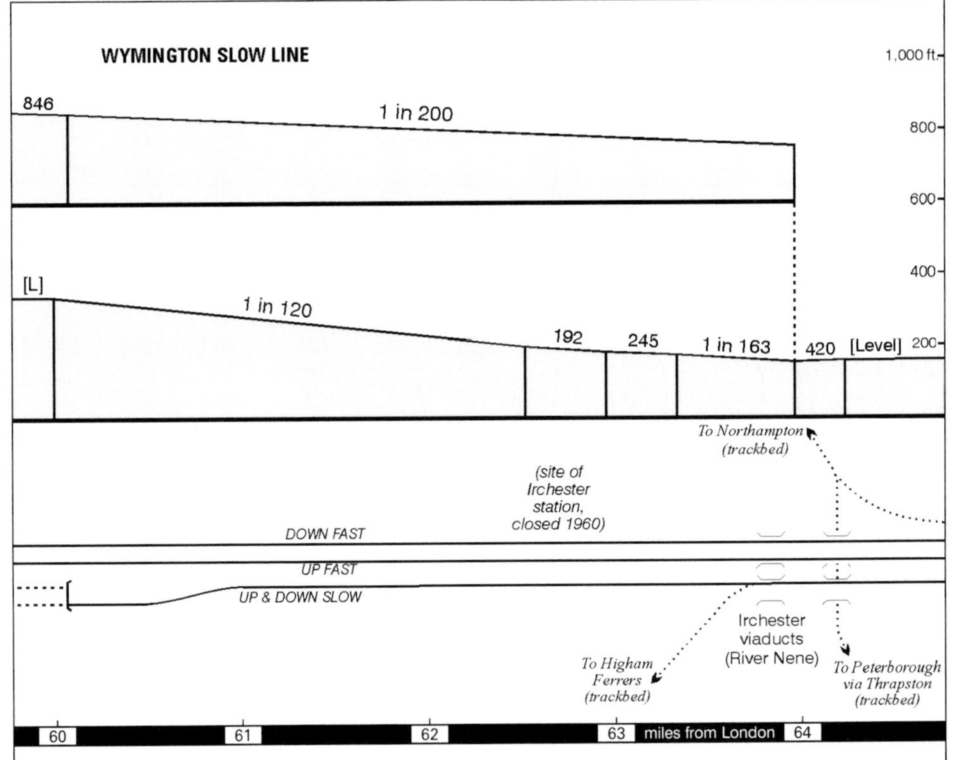

SHARNBROOK SUMMIT : The summit lies 315 ft. above sea level and is the location for another view of 60092, this time shortly after leaving Sharnbrook Tunnel on the Wymington deviation with 6V76, Stud Farm - Hayes Tarmac stone hoppers; the fast lines are above and to the left out of view. (NG 03/97)

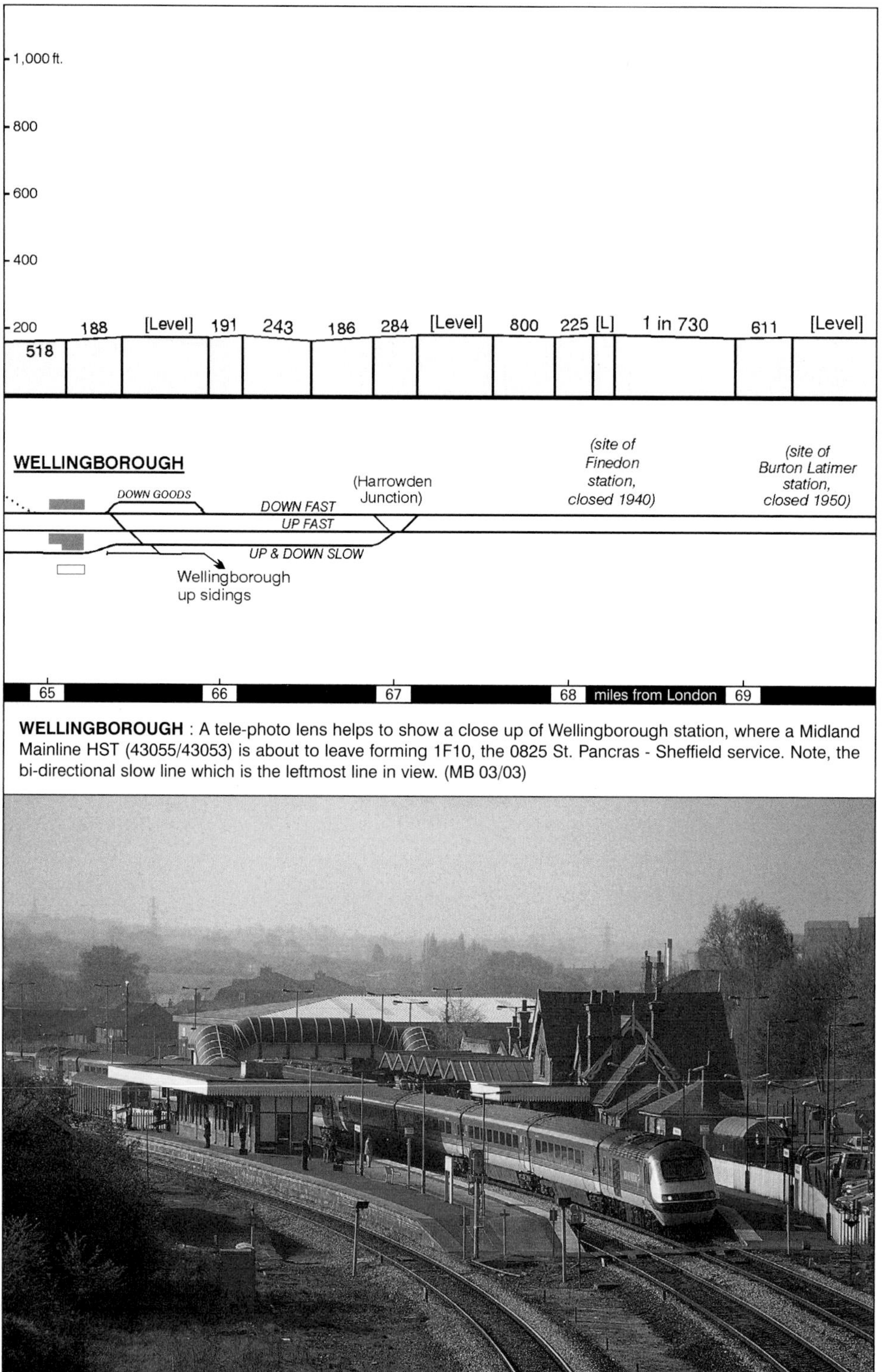

WELLINGBOROUGH : A tele-photo lens helps to show a close up of Wellingborough station, where a Midland Mainline HST (43055/43053) is about to leave forming 1F10, the 0825 St. Pancras - Sheffield service. Note, the bi-directional slow line which is the leftmost line in view. (MB 03/03)

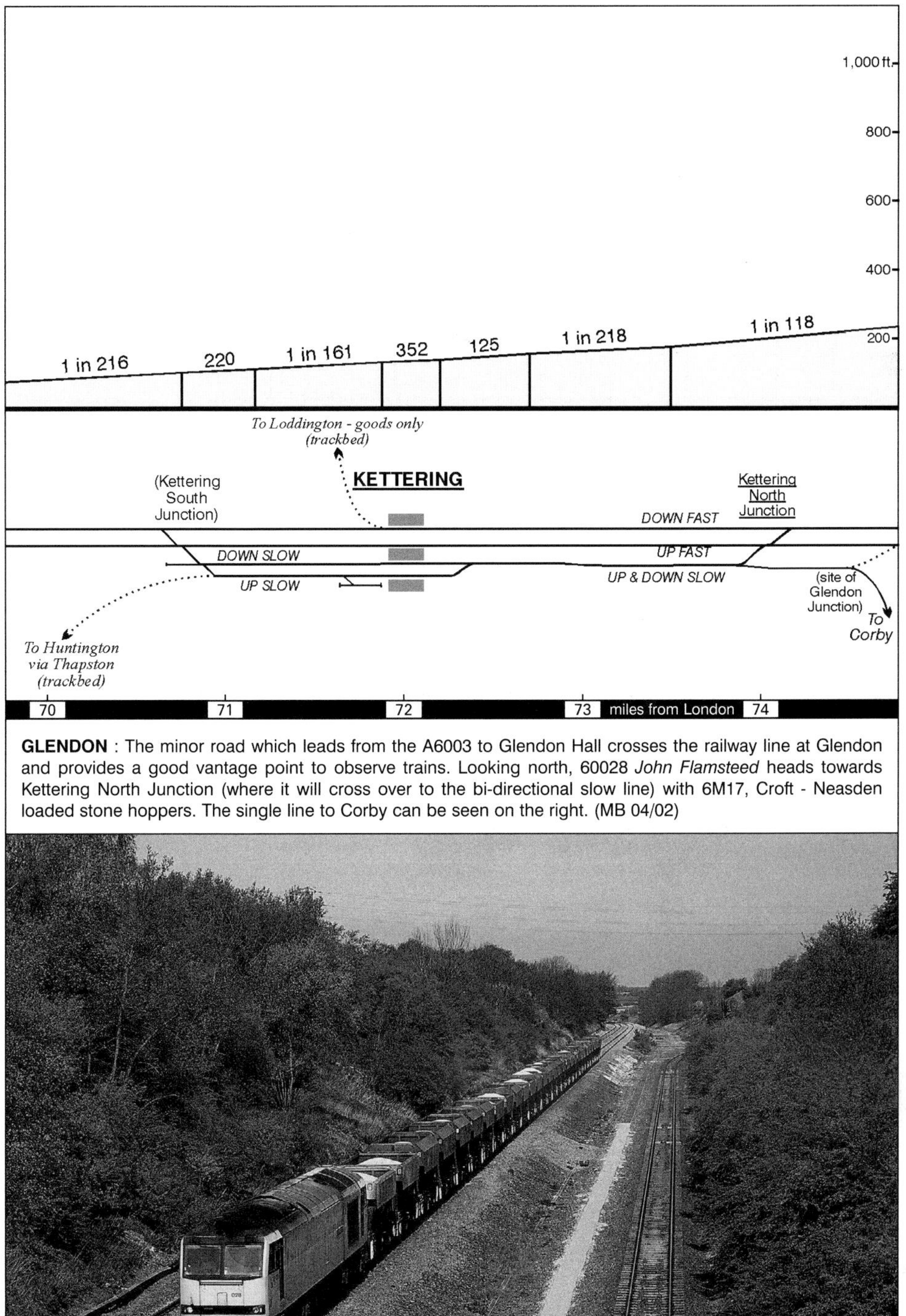

GLENDON : The minor road which leads from the A6003 to Glendon Hall crosses the railway line at Glendon and provides a good vantage point to observe trains. Looking north, 60028 *John Flamsteed* heads towards Kettering North Junction (where it will cross over to the bi-directional slow line) with 6M17, Croft - Neasden loaded stone hoppers. The single line to Corby can be seen on the right. (MB 04/02)

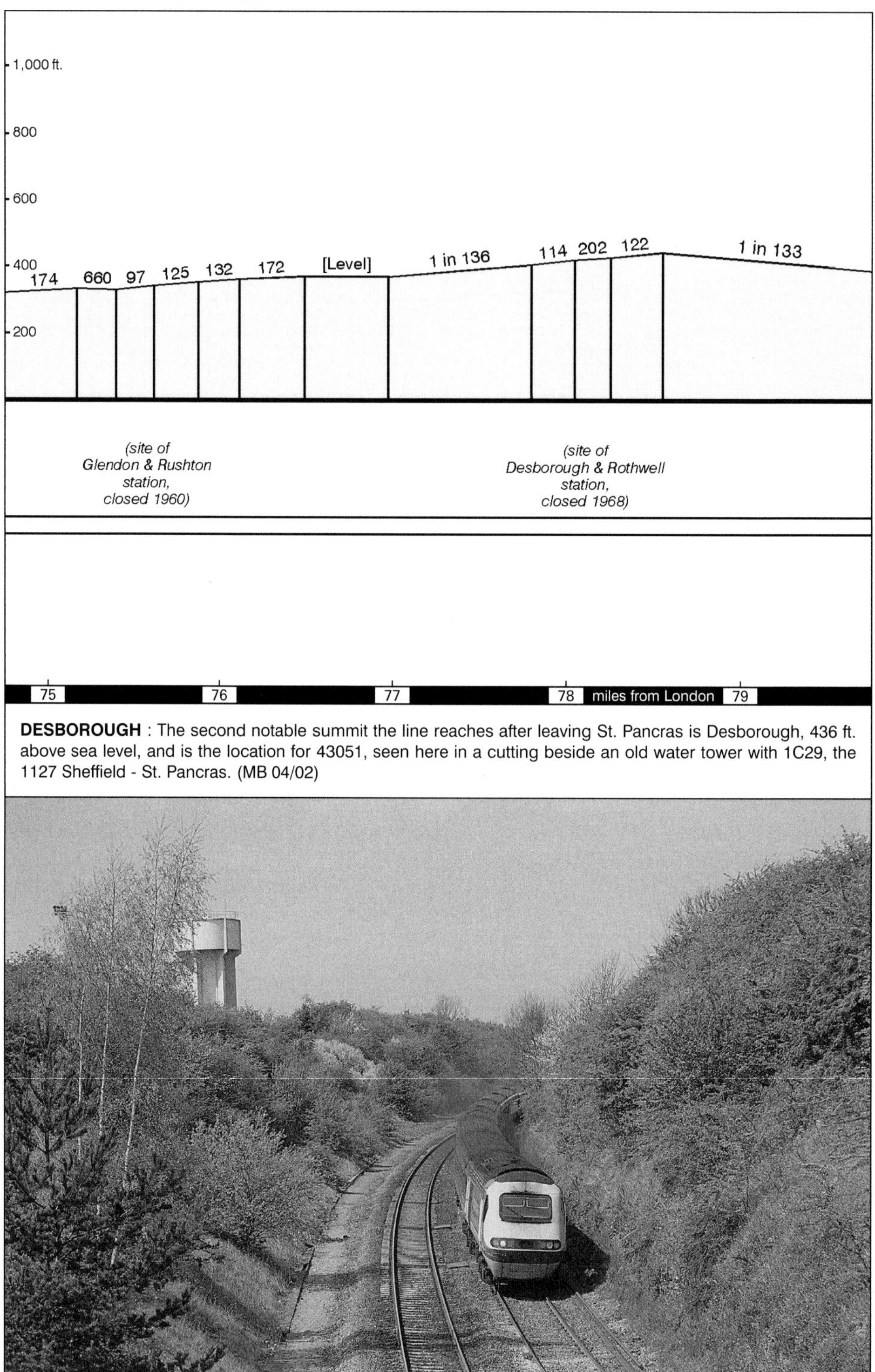

DESBOROUGH : The second notable summit the line reaches after leaving St. Pancras is Desborough, 436 ft. above sea level, and is the location for 43051, seen here in a cutting beside an old water tower with 1C29, the 1127 Sheffield - St. Pancras. (MB 04/02)

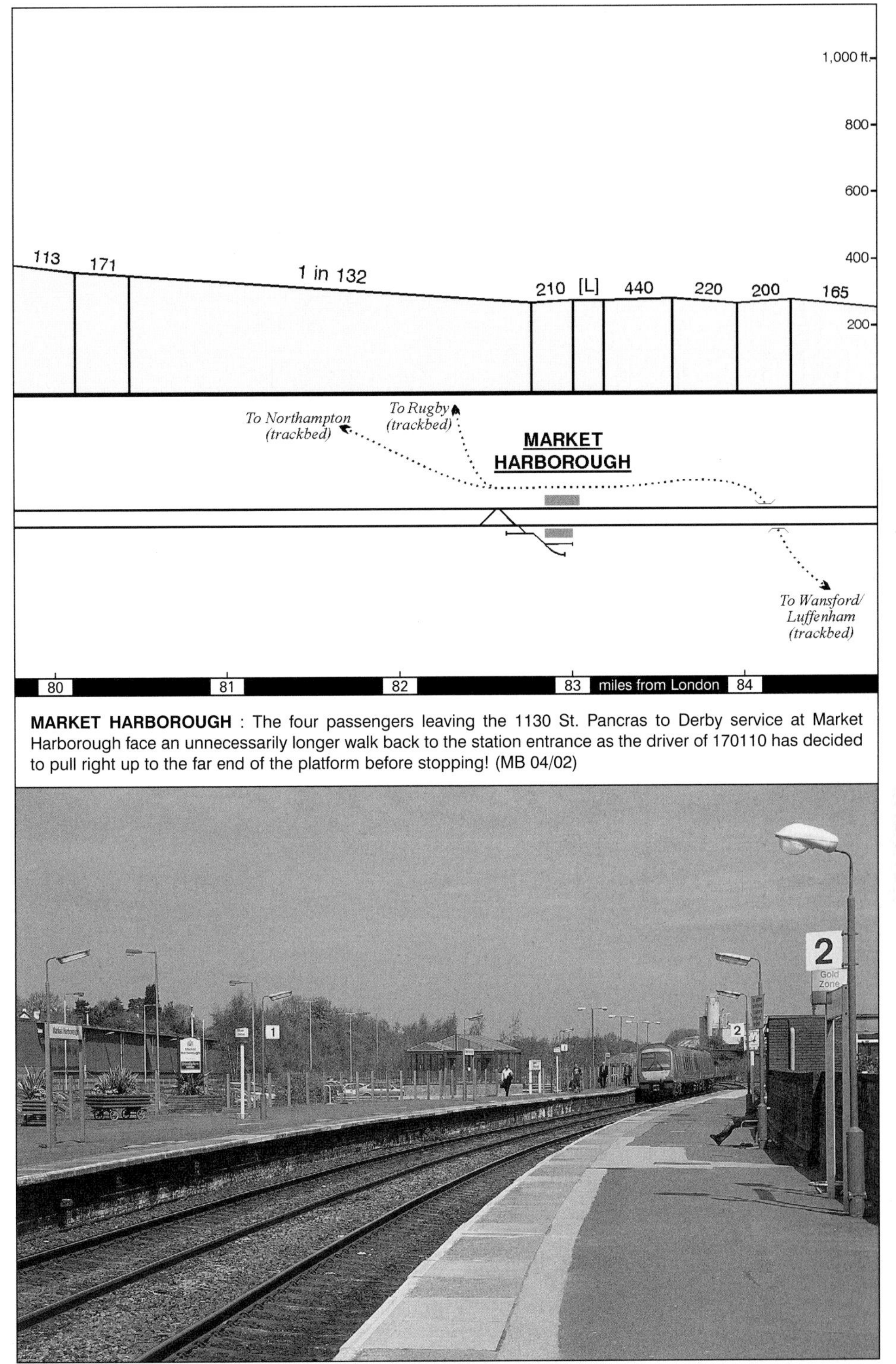

MARKET HARBOROUGH : The four passengers leaving the 1130 St. Pancras to Derby service at Market Harborough face an unnecessarily longer walk back to the station entrance as the driver of 170110 has decided to pull right up to the far end of the platform before stopping! (MB 04/02)

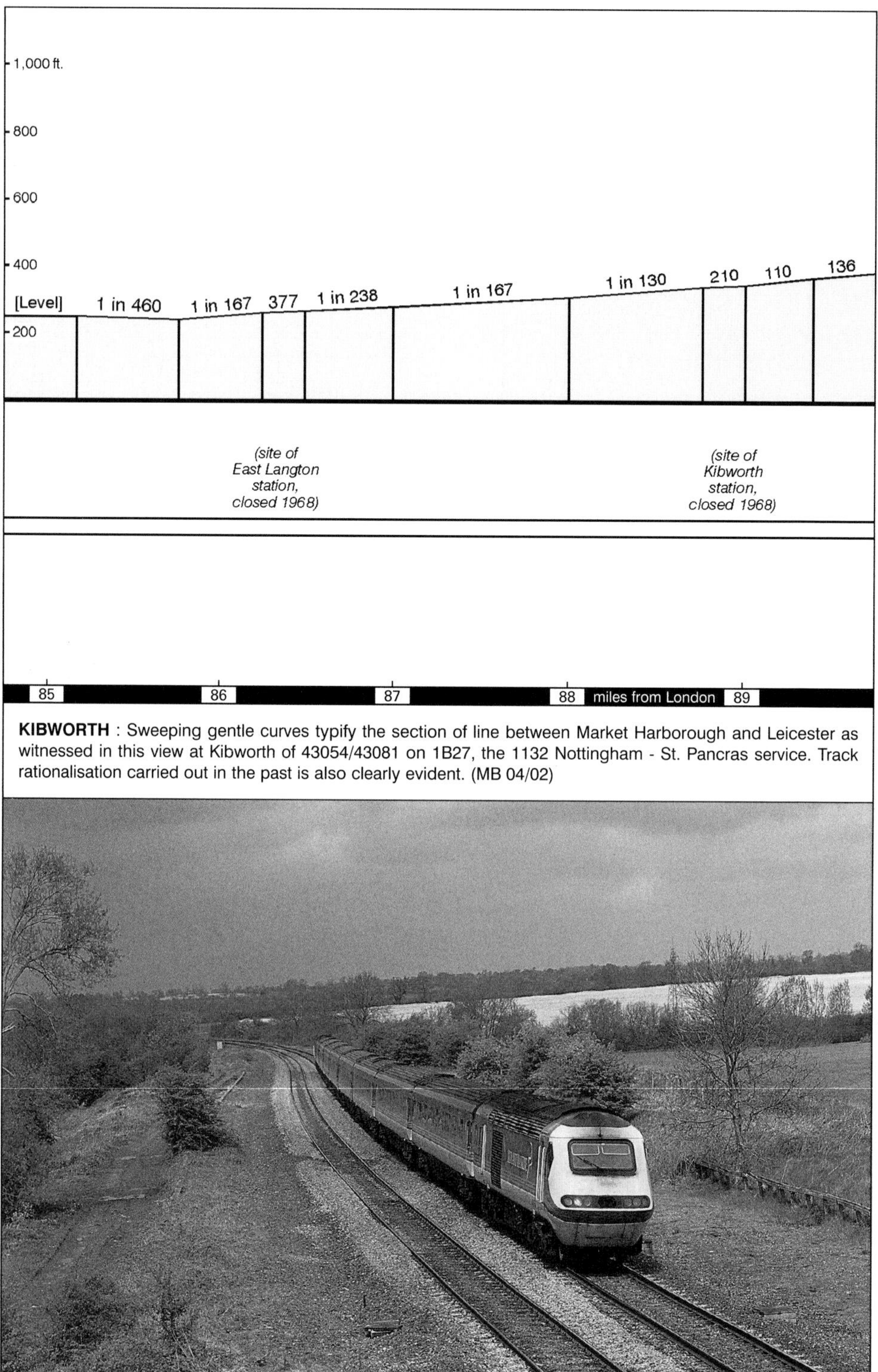

KIBWORTH : Sweeping gentle curves typify the section of line between Market Harborough and Leicester as witnessed in this view at Kibworth of 43054/43081 on 1B27, the 1132 Nottingham - St. Pancras service. Track rationalisation carried out in the past is also clearly evident. (MB 04/02)

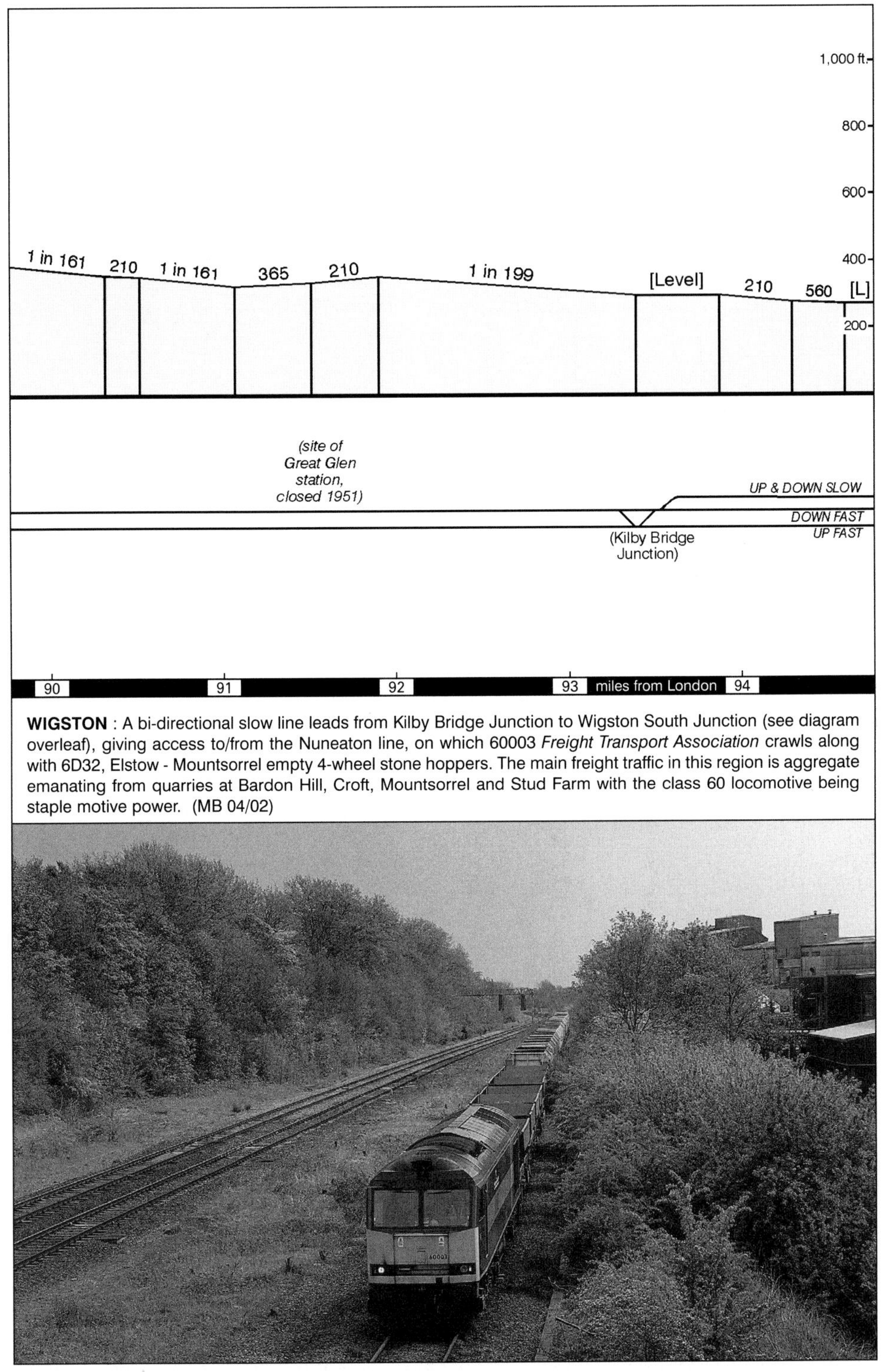

WIGSTON : A bi-directional slow line leads from Kilby Bridge Junction to Wigston South Junction (see diagram overleaf), giving access to/from the Nuneaton line, on which 60003 *Freight Transport Association* crawls along with 6D32, Elstow - Mountsorrel empty 4-wheel stone hoppers. The main freight traffic in this region is aggregate emanating from quarries at Bardon Hill, Croft, Mountsorrel and Stud Farm with the class 60 locomotive being staple motive power. (MB 04/02)

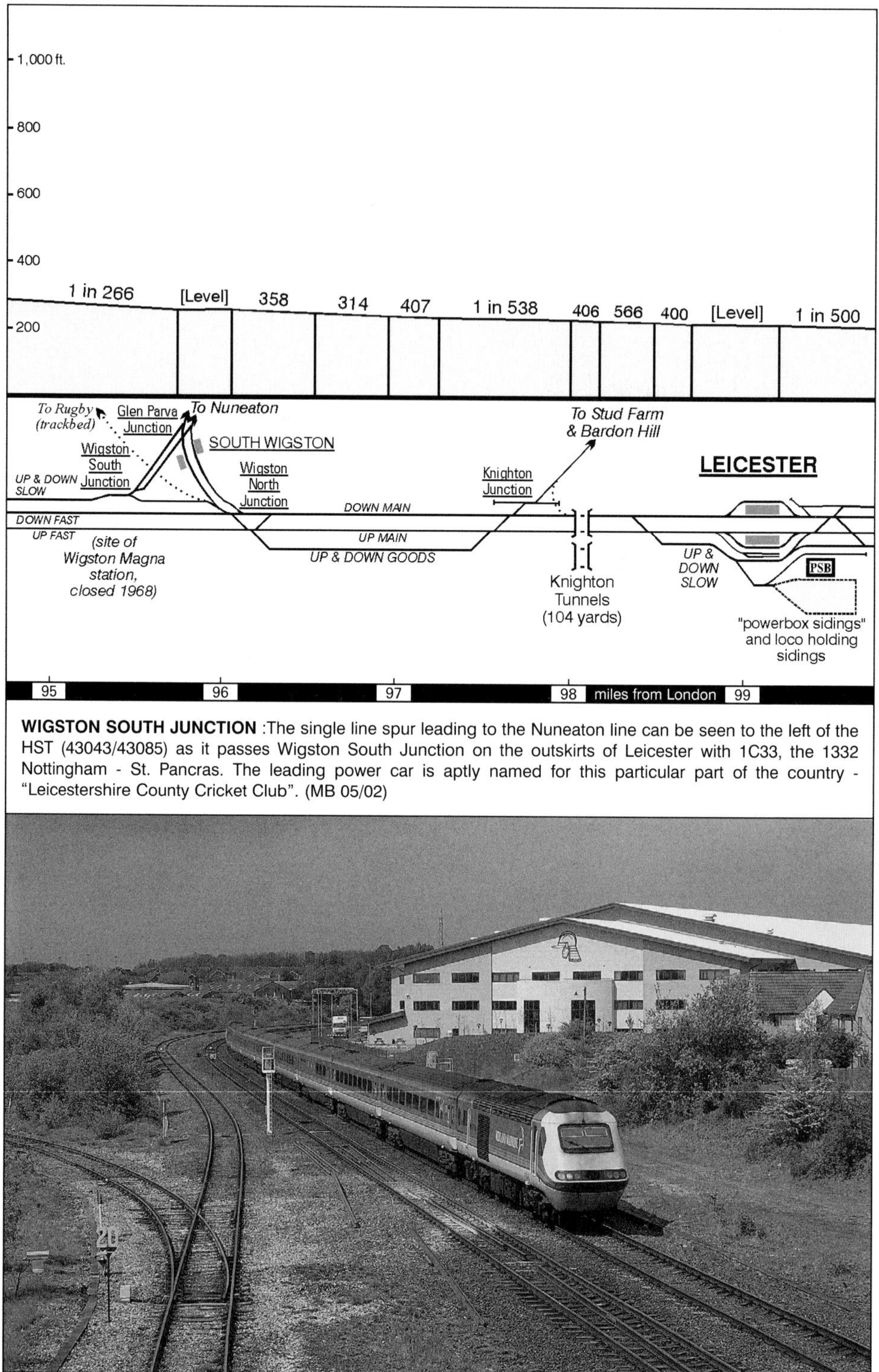

WIGSTON SOUTH JUNCTION :The single line spur leading to the Nuneaton line can be seen to the left of the HST (43043/43085) as it passes Wigston South Junction on the outskirts of Leicester with 1C33, the 1332 Nottingham - St. Pancras. The leading power car is aptly named for this particular part of the country - "Leicestershire County Cricket Club". (MB 05/02)

LEICESTER : The station at Leicester comprises of two island platforms, which can be seen to good effect in this view of an HST (*above*) ready to depart with 1F18, the 1025 St. Pancras - Sheffield.The leading power car is 43106 *Royal Philarmonic*. (MB 05/02)

The locomotive stabling & fuelling point is located to the North East of Leicester station on the 'up' side of the main line. On the fuelling point is 66208 (*below*) while the stabling point plays host to a rake of 4-wheel stone hoppers and withdrawn 58005 *Ironbridge Power Station*. (MB 05/02)

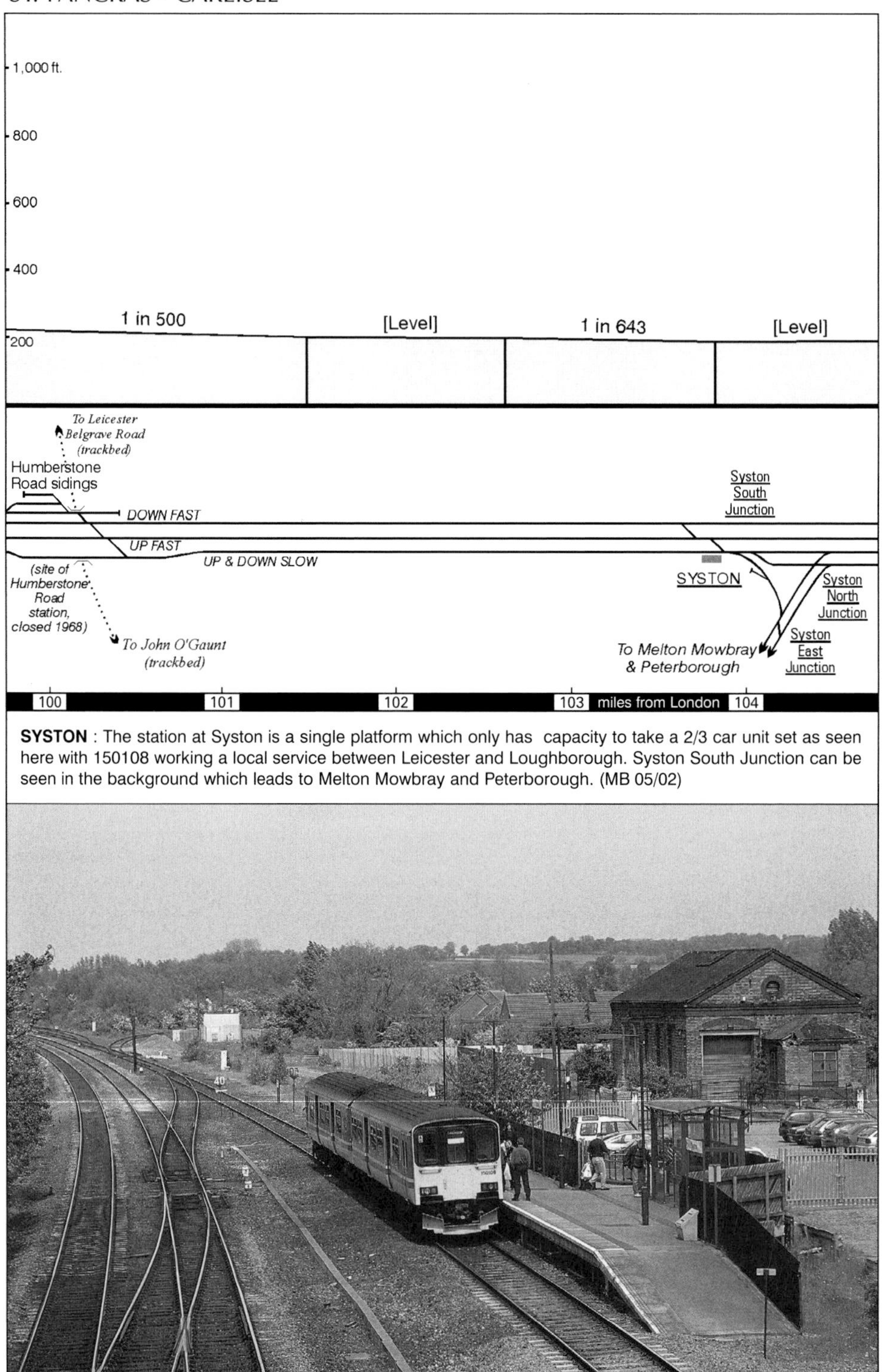

SYSTON : The station at Syston is a single platform which only has capacity to take a 2/3 car unit set as seen here with 150108 working a local service between Leicester and Loughborough. Syston South Junction can be seen in the background which leads to Melton Mowbray and Peterborough. (MB 05/02)

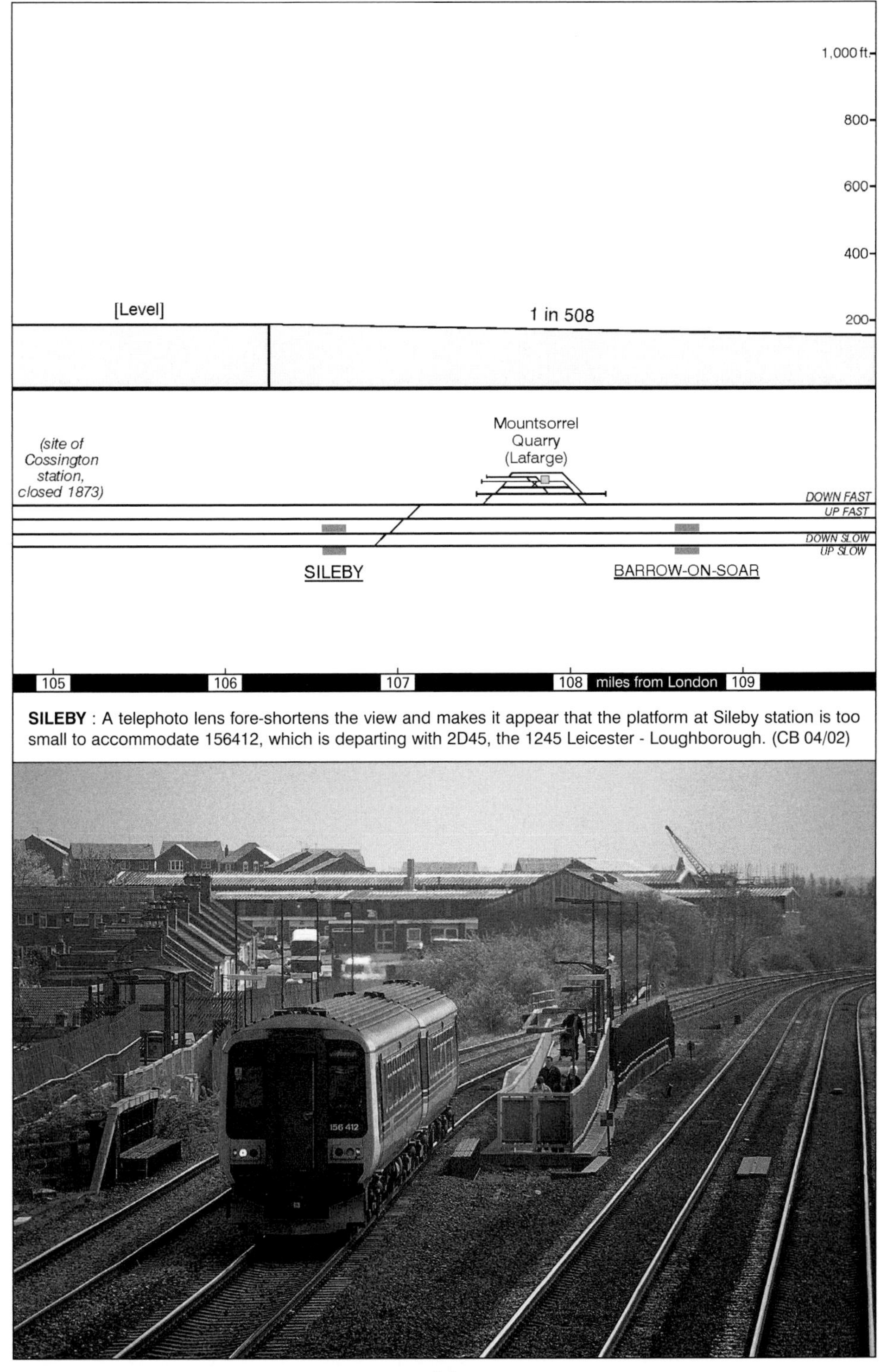

SILEBY : A telephoto lens fore-shortens the view and makes it appear that the platform at Sileby station is too small to accommodate 156412, which is departing with 2D45, the 1245 Leicester - Loughborough. (CB 04/02)

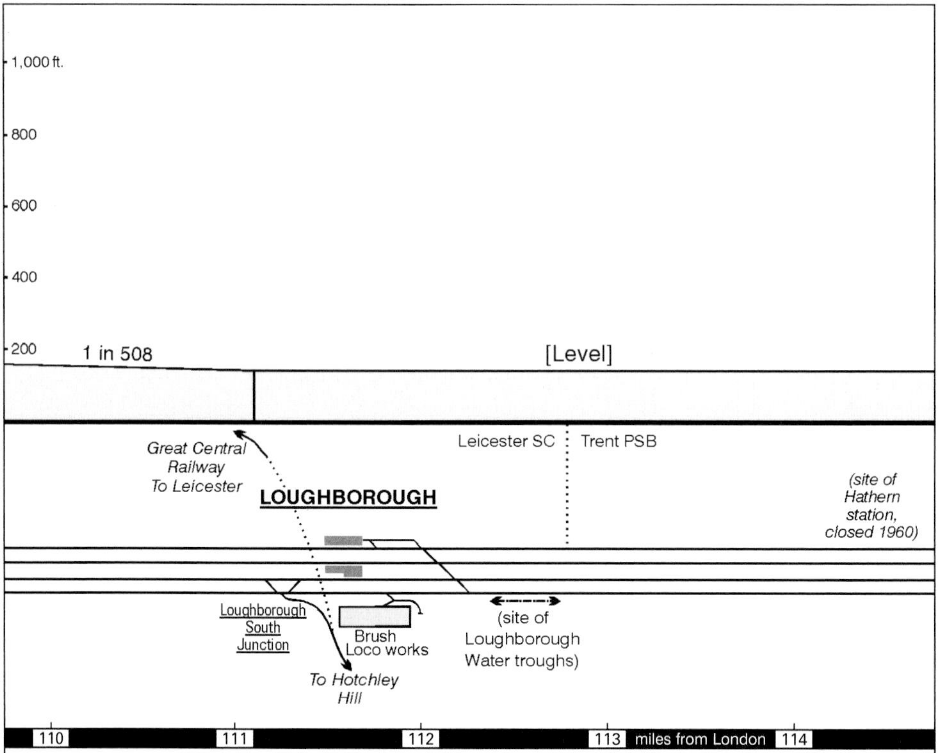

1,000 ft.
800
600
400
200

1 in 508
[Level]

Great Central Railway To Leicester
LOUGHBOROUGH
Leicester SC
Trent PSB
(site of Hathern station, closed 1960)
Loughborough South Junction
Brush Loco works
(site of Loughborough Water troughs)
To Hotchley Hill

110 111 112 113 miles from London 114

LOUGHBOROUGH : The station is visible in the distance as 66147 passes Loughborough on the northbound goods line with 4P37, the 1400 Rugeley power station - Toton, formed of empty HTA wagons. Part of Brush Locomotive Works is visible in the background although, as can be seen, some of the site's land has been sold off and redeveloped; hence the bright new buildings!. (PC 08/02)

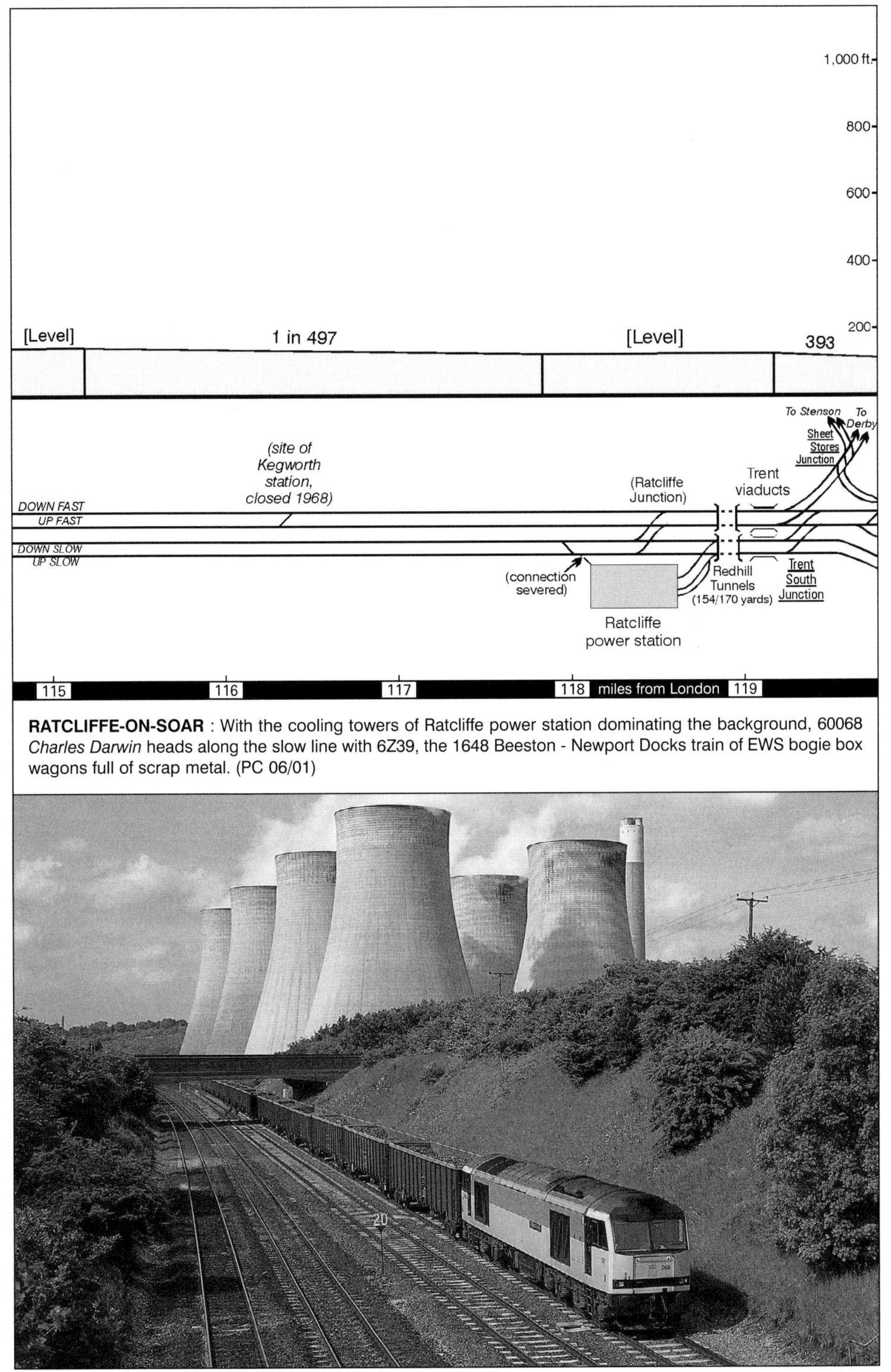

RATCLIFFE-ON-SOAR : With the cooling towers of Ratcliffe power station dominating the background, 60068 *Charles Darwin* heads along the slow line with 6Z39, the 1648 Beeston - Newport Docks train of EWS bogie box wagons full of scrap metal. (PC 06/01)

TOTON CENTRE : The marshalling yards are ostensibly used to stage MGR coal trains operating between coalfields and power stations in the East Midlands and the depot is EWSR's main motive power depot - one of the biggest in Europe. A panoramic view sees 37798 (*above*) light engine at Toton with Ratcliffe power station dominating the skyline. (CB 08/02)

Photographed from 'the bank' alongside Toton, 56112 (*below*) awaits departure with 6T21, the 1050 Toton - Hicks Lodge MGR empties. These five former dead-end sidings had only recently been brought back into use having been used for storing scrap locomotives. (PC 06/02)

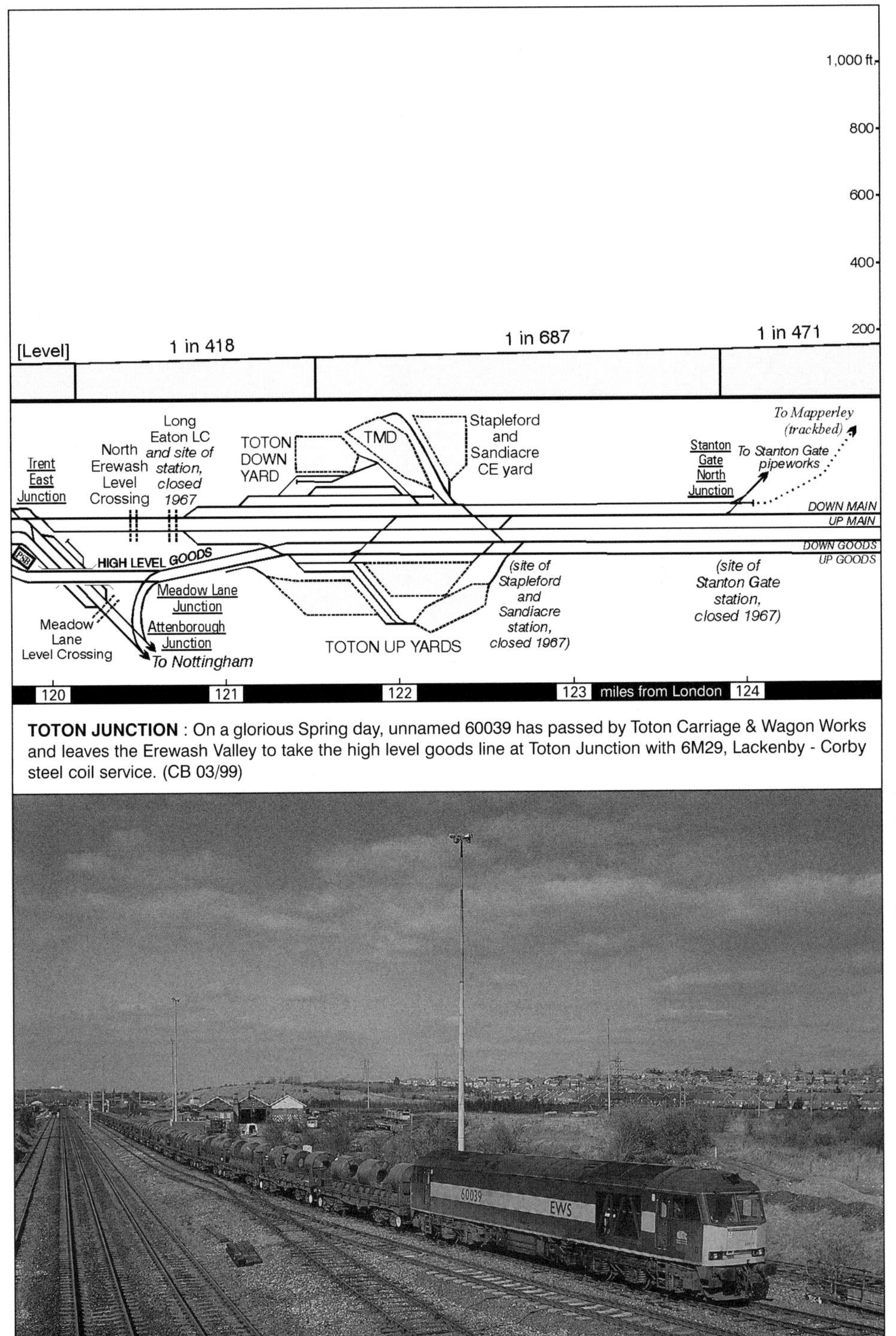

TOTON JUNCTION : On a glorious Spring day, unnamed 60039 has passed by Toton Carriage & Wagon Works and leaves the Erewash Valley to take the high level goods line at Toton Junction with 6M29, Lackenby - Corby steel coil service. (CB 03/99)

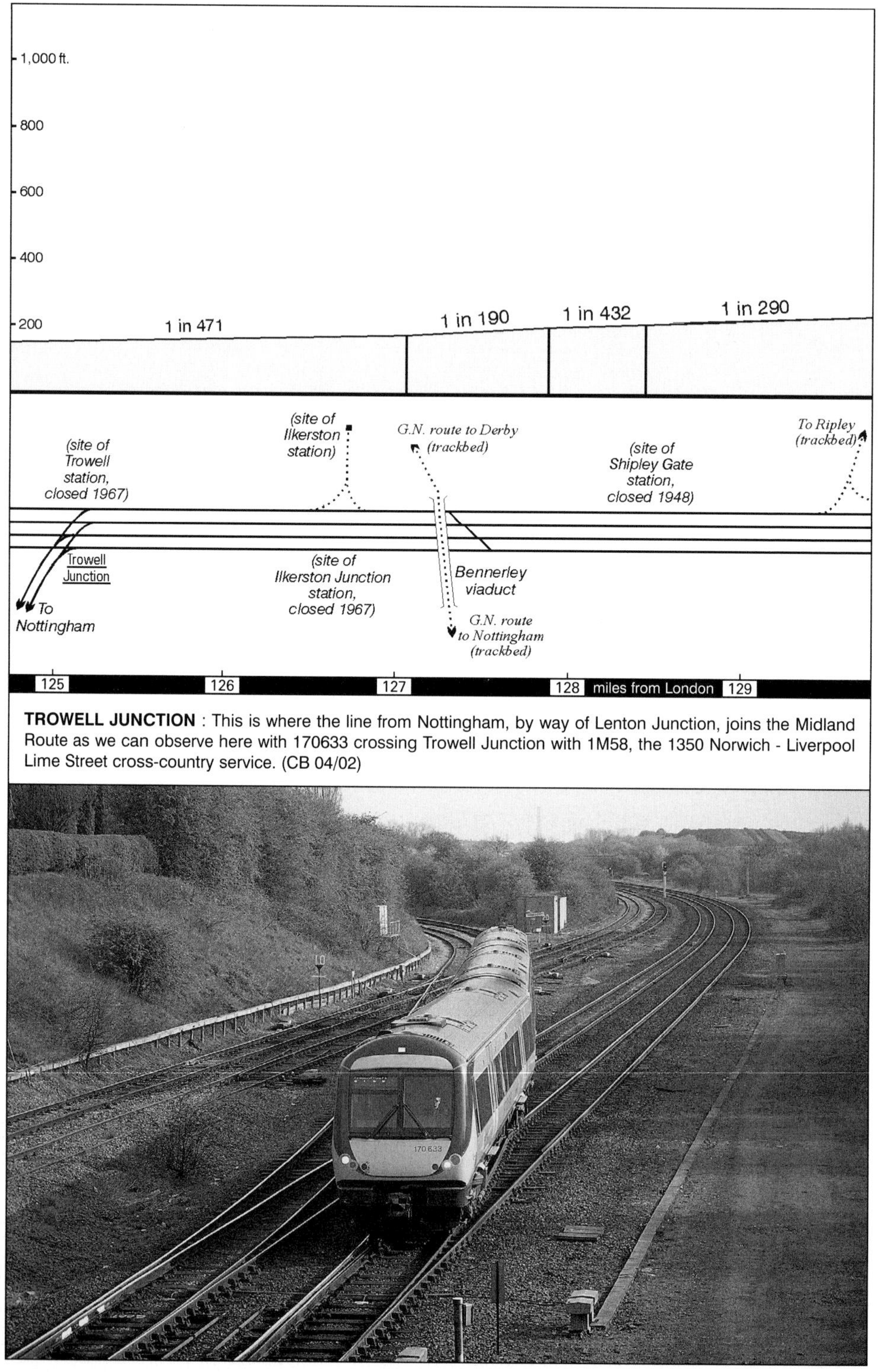

TROWELL JUNCTION : This is where the line from Nottingham, by way of Lenton Junction, joins the Midland Route as we can observe here with 170633 crossing Trowell Junction with 1M58, the 1350 Norwich - Liverpool Lime Street cross-country service. (CB 04/02)

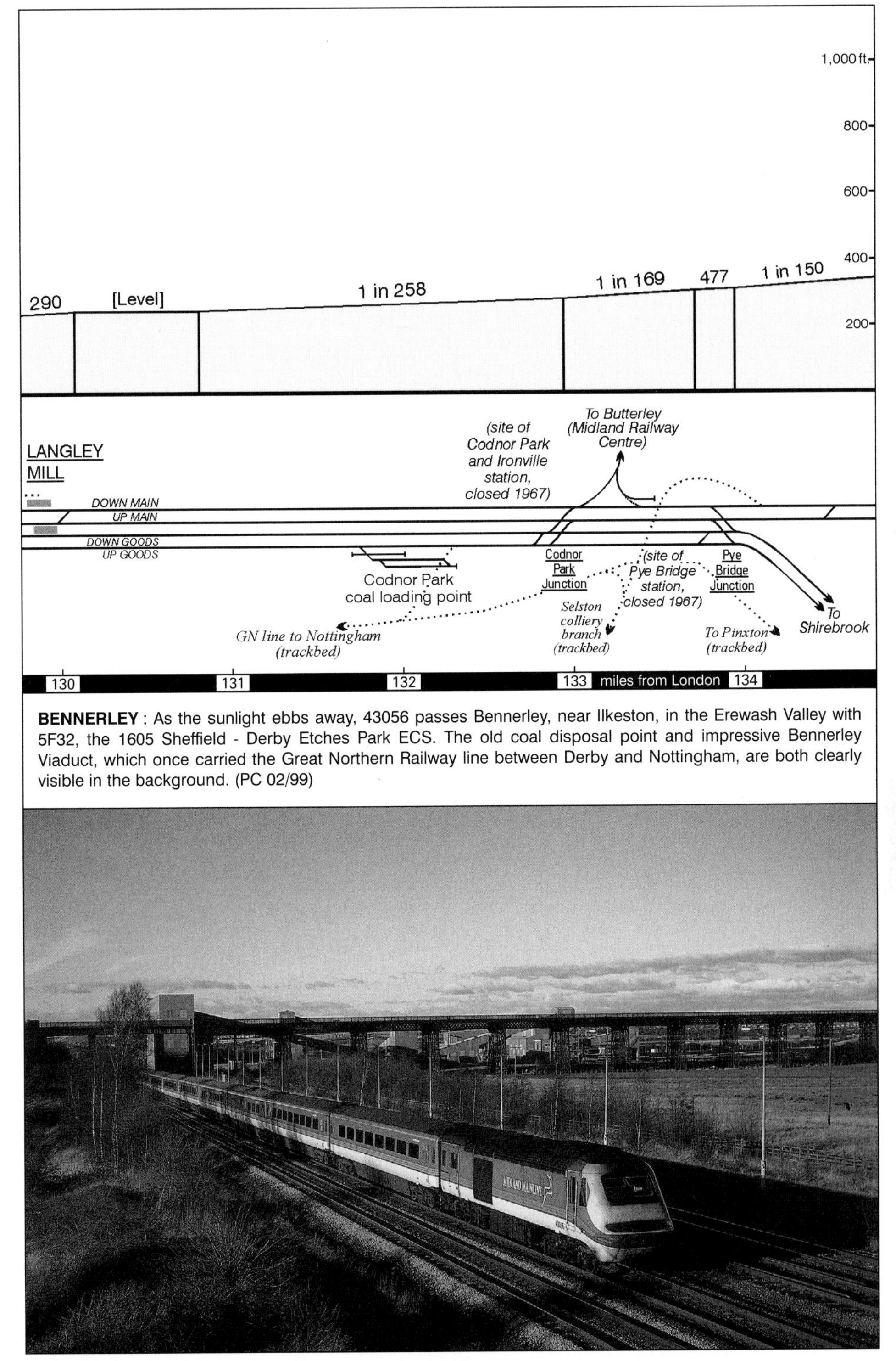

BENNERLEY : As the sunlight ebbs away, 43056 passes Bennerley, near Ilkeston, in the Erewash Valley with 5F32, the 1605 Sheffield - Derby Etches Park ECS. The old coal disposal point and impressive Bennerley Viaduct, which once carried the Great Northern Railway line between Derby and Nottingham, are both clearly visible in the background. (PC 02/99)

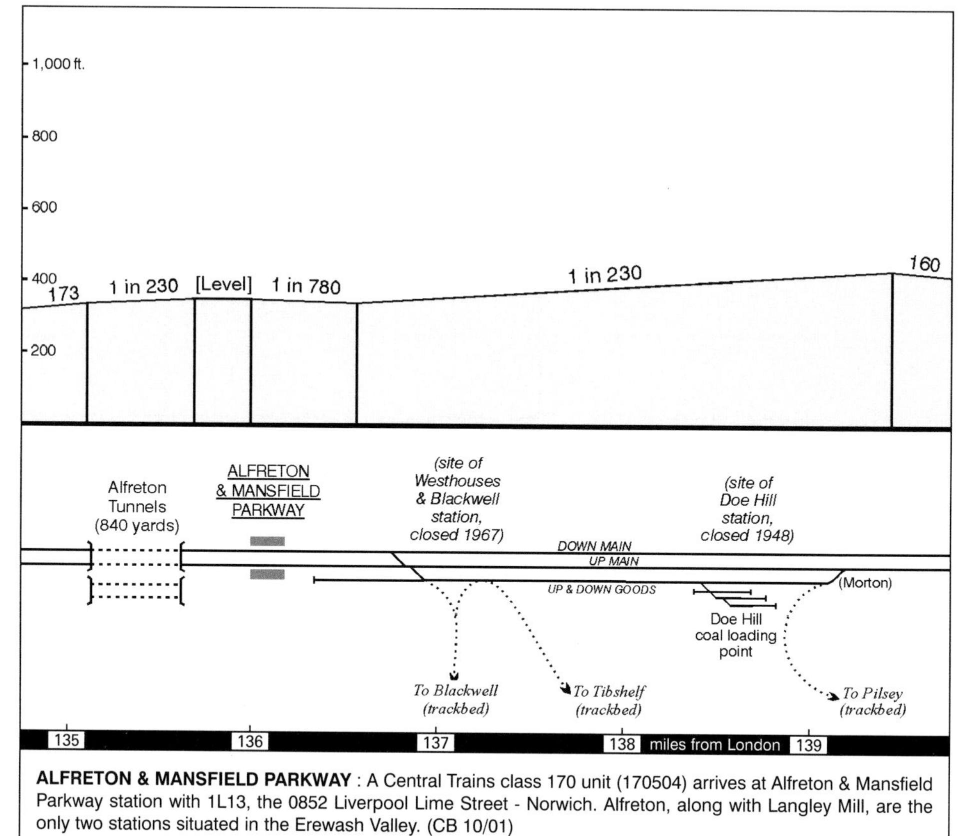

ALFRETON & MANSFIELD PARKWAY : A Central Trains class 170 unit (170504) arrives at Alfreton & Mansfield Parkway station with 1L13, the 0852 Liverpool Lime Street - Norwich. Alfreton, along with Langley Mill, are the only two stations situated in the Erewash Valley. (CB 10/01)

CLAY CROSS SOUTH JUNCTION : This is where the lines through the Erewash valley meet up with the main line from Derby. At the junction, 66226 heads northwards with 6T14, a special working of empty EWS coal hoppers from Toton to Milford. (CB 10/01)

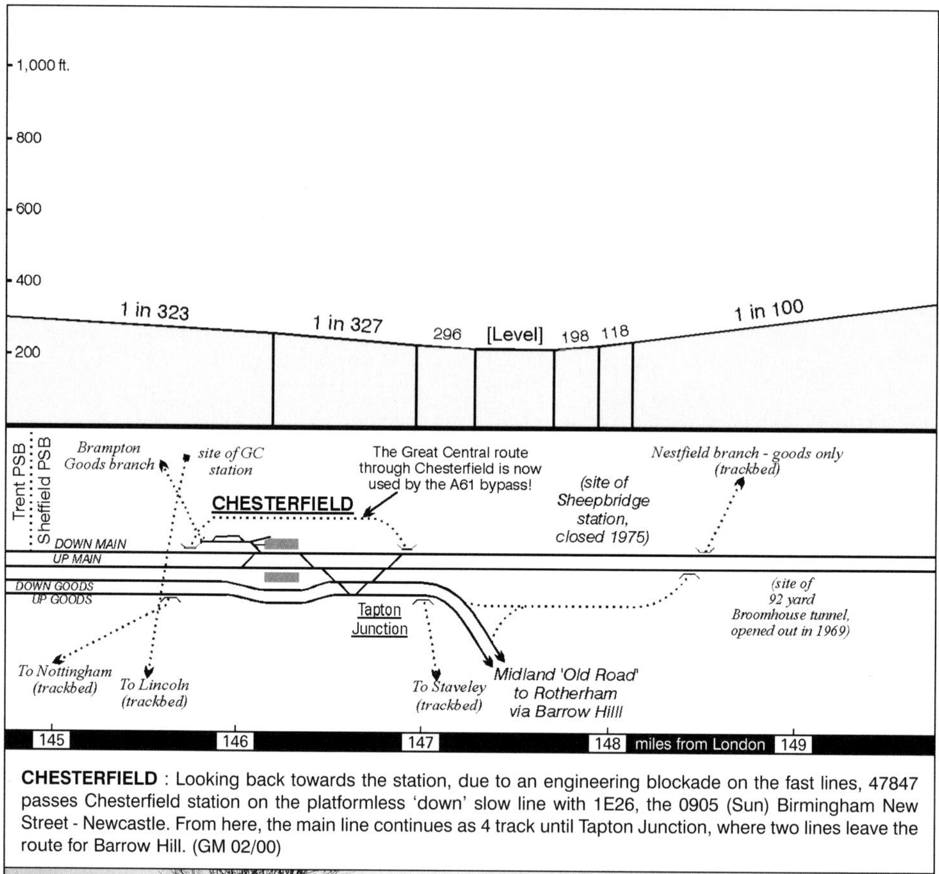

CHESTERFIELD : Looking back towards the station, due to an engineering blockade on the fast lines, 47847 passes Chesterfield station on the platformless 'down' slow line with 1E26, the 0905 (Sun) Birmingham New Street - Newcastle. From here, the main line continues as 4 track until Tapton Junction, where two lines leave the route for Barrow Hill. (GM 02/00)

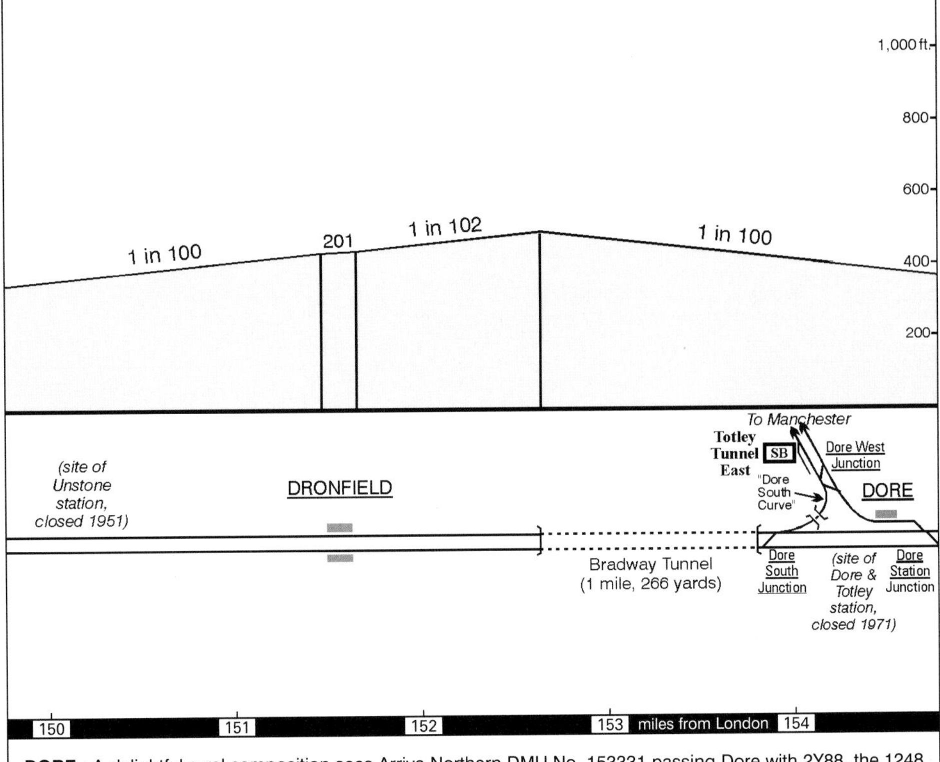

DORE : A delightful rural composition sees Arriva Northern DMU No. 153331 passing Dore with 2Y88, the 1248 Sheffield - Chesterfield. The station at Dore is actually not on the Midland Route, but on a single line spur which leads from Dore Station Junction to Dore West Junction and thence the Hope valley. (CB 10/01)

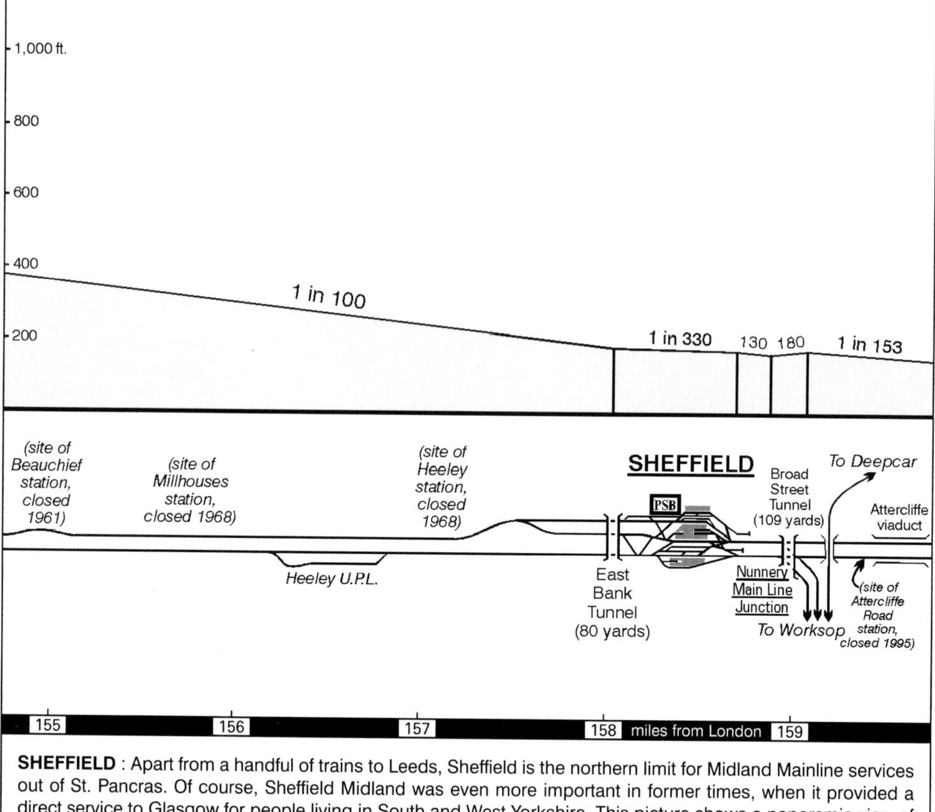

SHEFFIELD : Apart from a handful of trains to Leeds, Sheffield is the northern limit for Midland Mainline services out of St. Pancras. Of course, Sheffield Midland was even more important in former times, when it provided a direct service to Glasgow for people living in South and West Yorkshire. This picture shows a panoramic view of the northern end of the station where 144016 is involved in a positioning move between platforms in readiness for its next service. (CB 06/02)

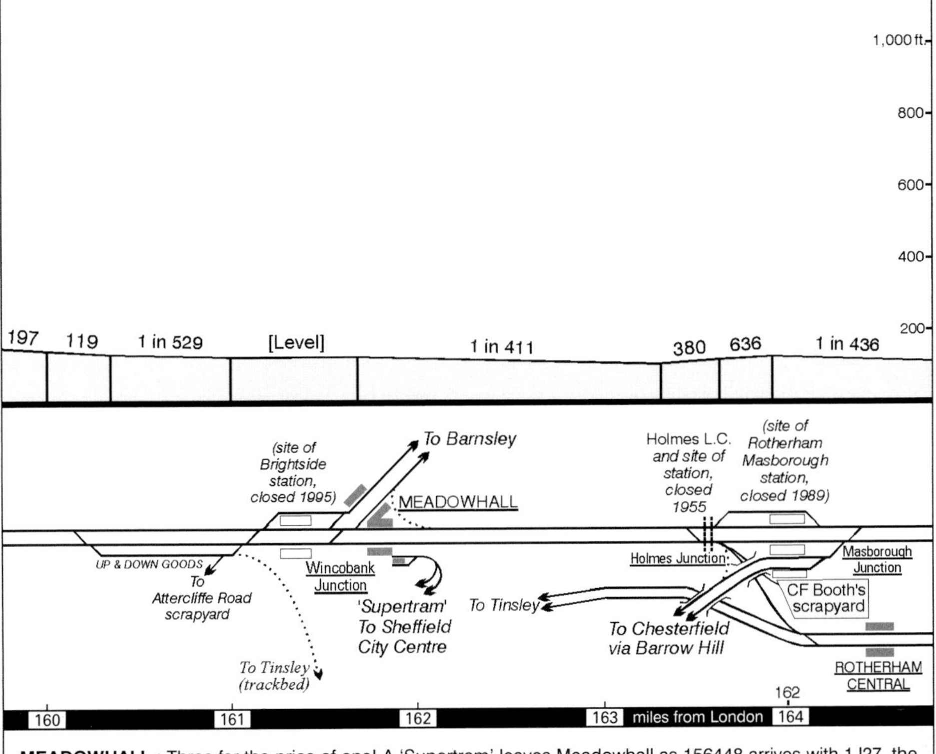

MEADOWHALL : Three for the price of one! A 'Supertram' leaves Meadowhall as 156448 arrives with 1J27, the 0716 Bridlington - Sheffield, passing 158769 heading in the opposite direction on 2Y18, the 0918 Sheffield - Leeds. Of course, Meadowhall's main claim to fame is the massive shopping complex which was built on land once home to some of Sheffield's finest steel mills. (CB 06/02)

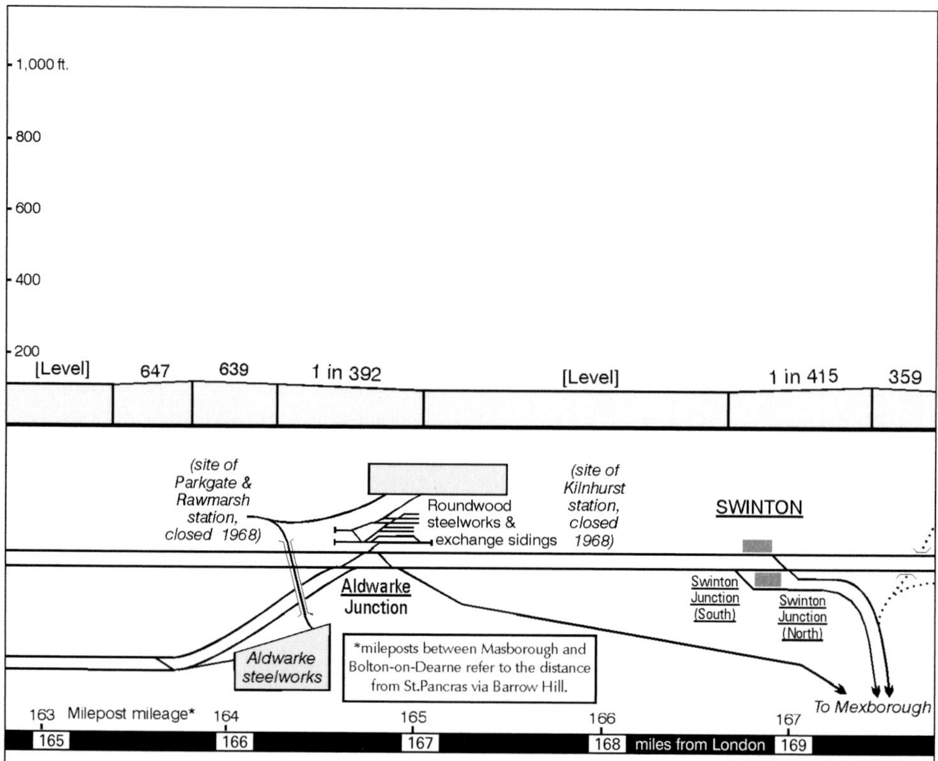

KILNHURST : Freightliner *Heavy Haul* moved swiftly into the imported coal sector to compete with EWS and, within two years of operating, had secured around 25% of the total market. Here, at Kilnhurst, one of their trains is illustrated in the shape of 66517 hauling 6G30, the 0650 Immingham - Rugeley power station, formed of the Company's own purpose built wagons. (CB 04/02)

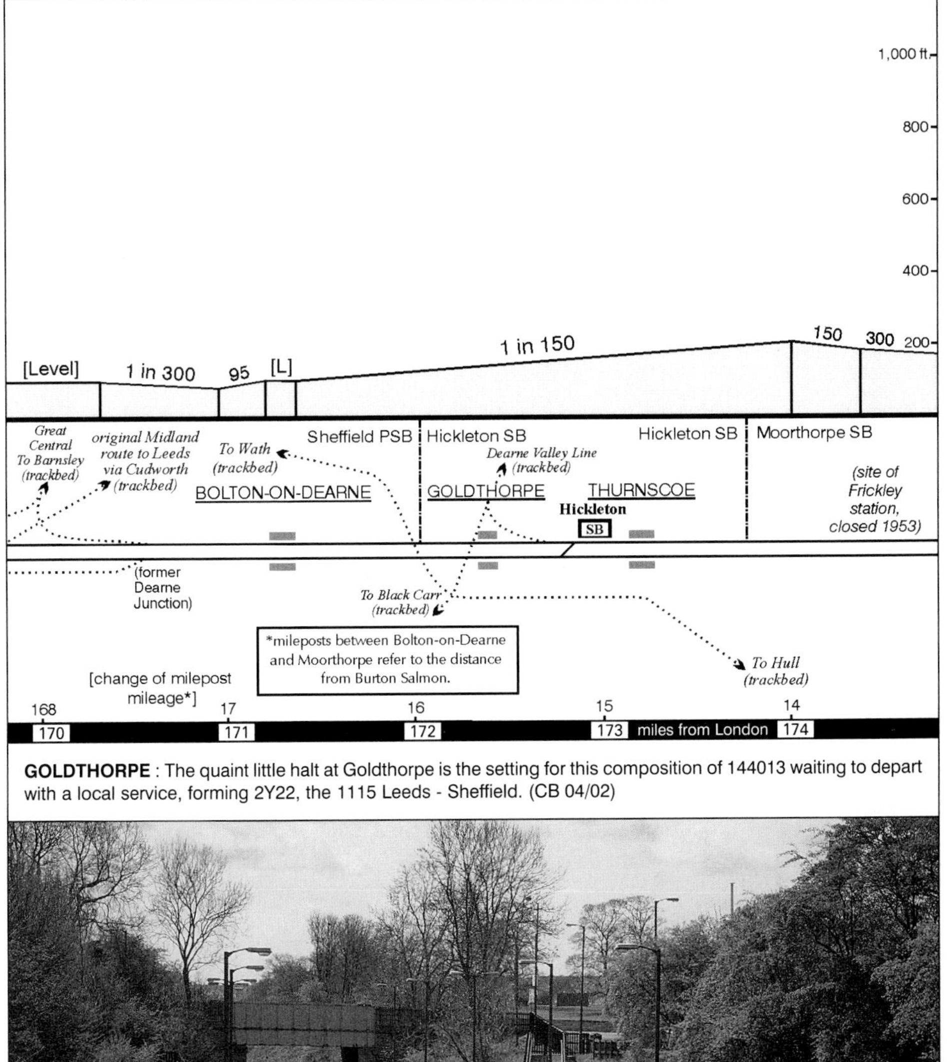

GOLDTHORPE : The quaint little halt at Goldthorpe is the setting for this composition of 144013 waiting to depart with a local service, forming 2Y22, the 1115 Leeds - Sheffield. (CB 04/02)

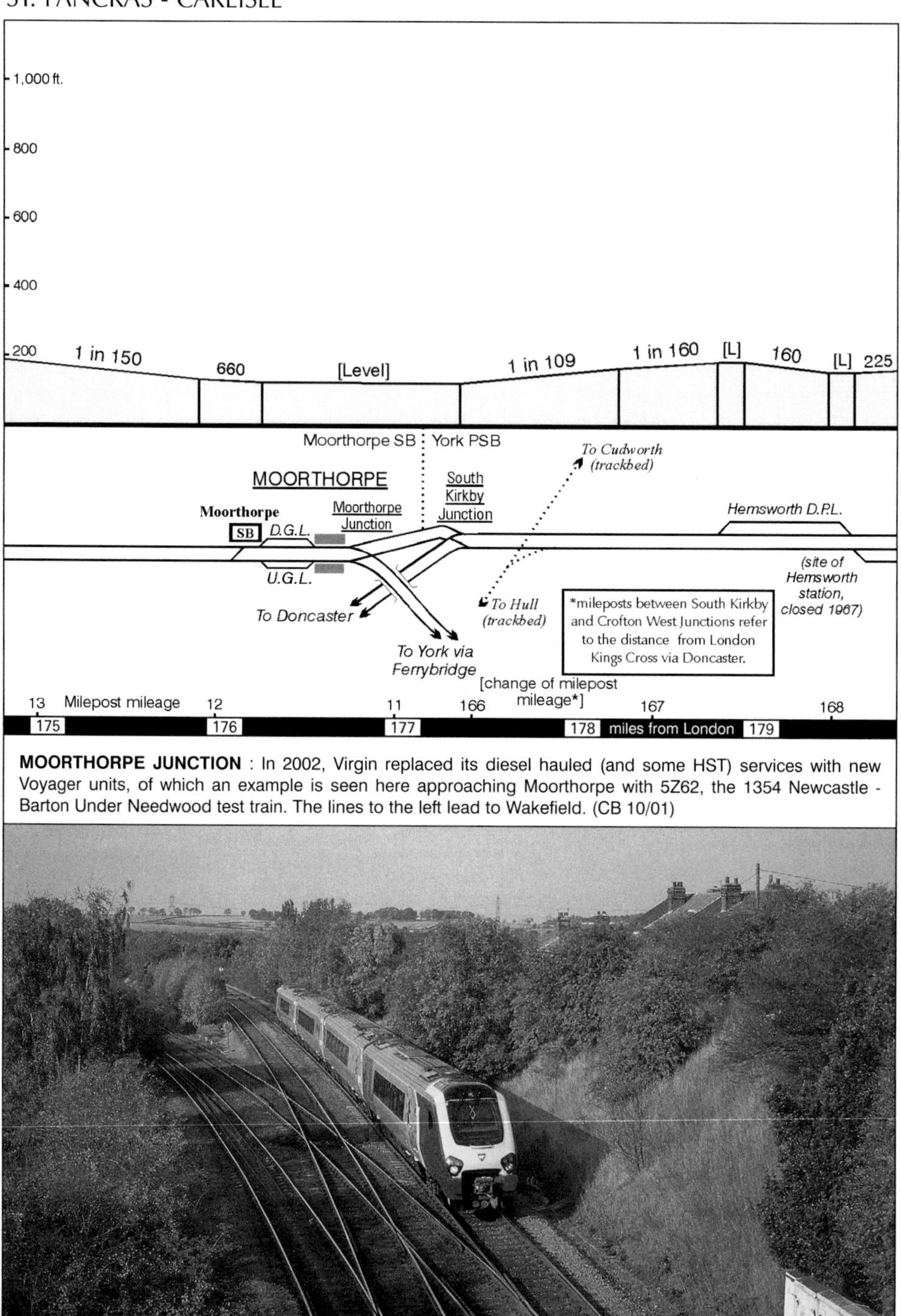

MOORTHORPE JUNCTION : In 2002, Virgin replaced its diesel hauled (and some HST) services with new Voyager units, of which an example is seen here approaching Moorthorpe with 5Z62, the 1354 Newcastle - Barton Under Needwood test train. The lines to the left lead to Wakefield. (CB 10/01)

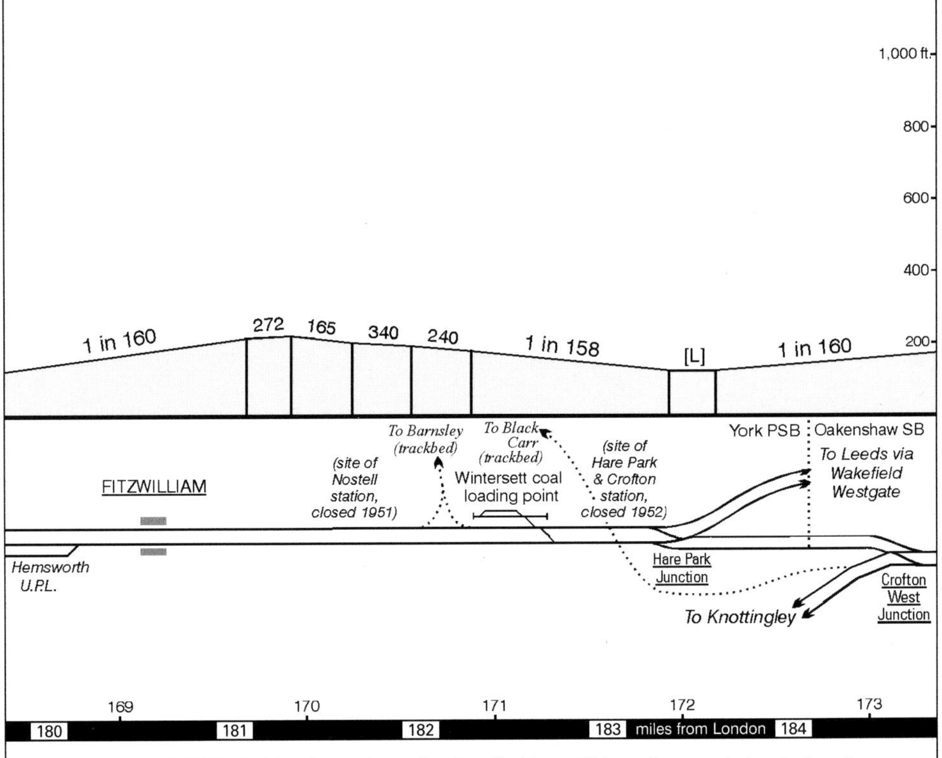

HARE PARK JUNCTION : At this point, we leave the electrified line, which continues on to Leeds, to gain access to Calder Bridge Junction and thence Normanton. At the junction itself, 43064 heads south to Doncaster and it's next station stop with 1C17, the 0725 Leeds - St. Pancras. (CB 05/02)

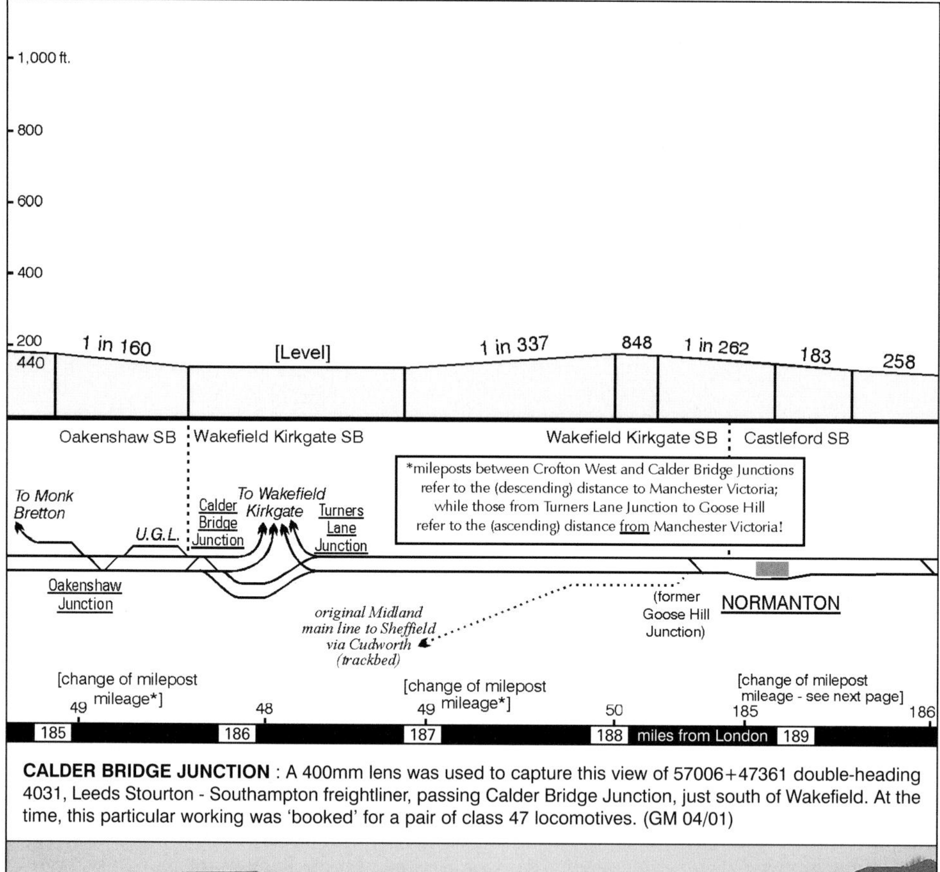

CALDER BRIDGE JUNCTION : A 400mm lens was used to capture this view of 57006+47361 double-heading 4031, Leeds Stourton - Southampton freightliner, passing Calder Bridge Junction, just south of Wakefield. At the time, this particular working was 'booked' for a pair of class 47 locomotives. (GM 04/01)

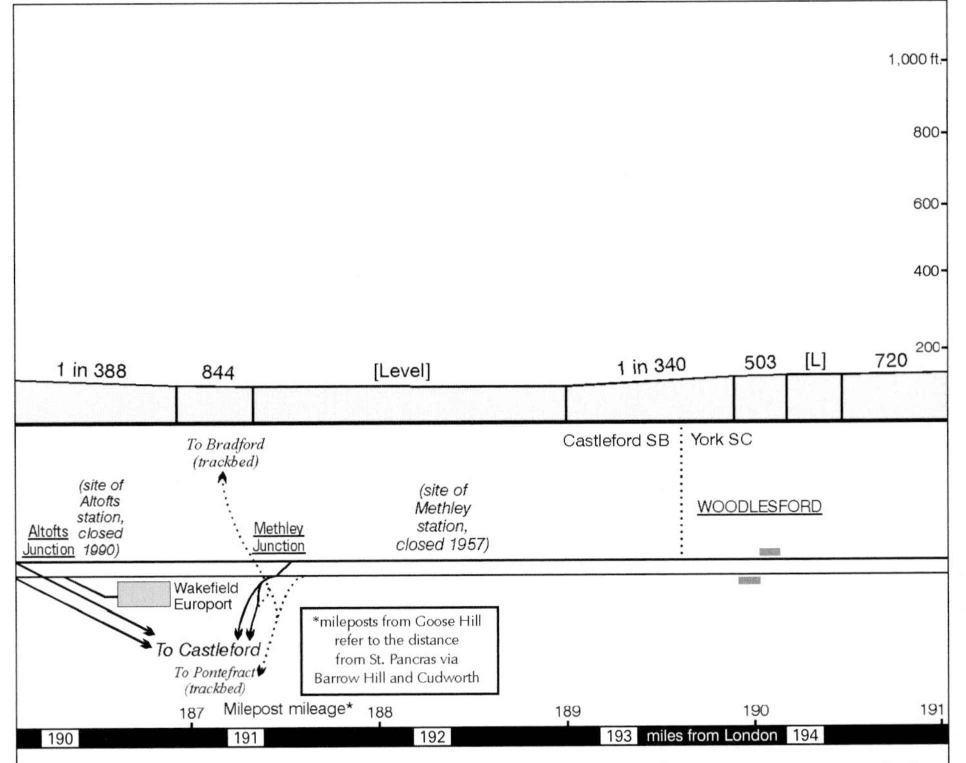

GOOSE HILL JUNCTION : This location has changed radically in appearance over the years; gone is the signalbox, semaphore signals and network of points. In the cutting, looking back towards Normanton, 43087+43070 pass the site of Goose Hill Junction with 1V60, the 1110 Edinburgh - Exeter St. Davids Virgin cross-country service during Sunday diversions via Normanton and Barnsley. (CB 05/02)

STOURTON : Leeds Freightliner Terminal is situated adjacent to the 'down' side of the main line , where 47287 (*above*) can be seen having arrived with a trainload of containers from the south. (GM 12/99)

Looking in the opposite direction, a class 08 shunter marshals a freightliner train while 66179 (*below*) passes with 6D48, Rylstone - Dewsbury stone, conveyed in EWS box wagons. (CB 10/02)

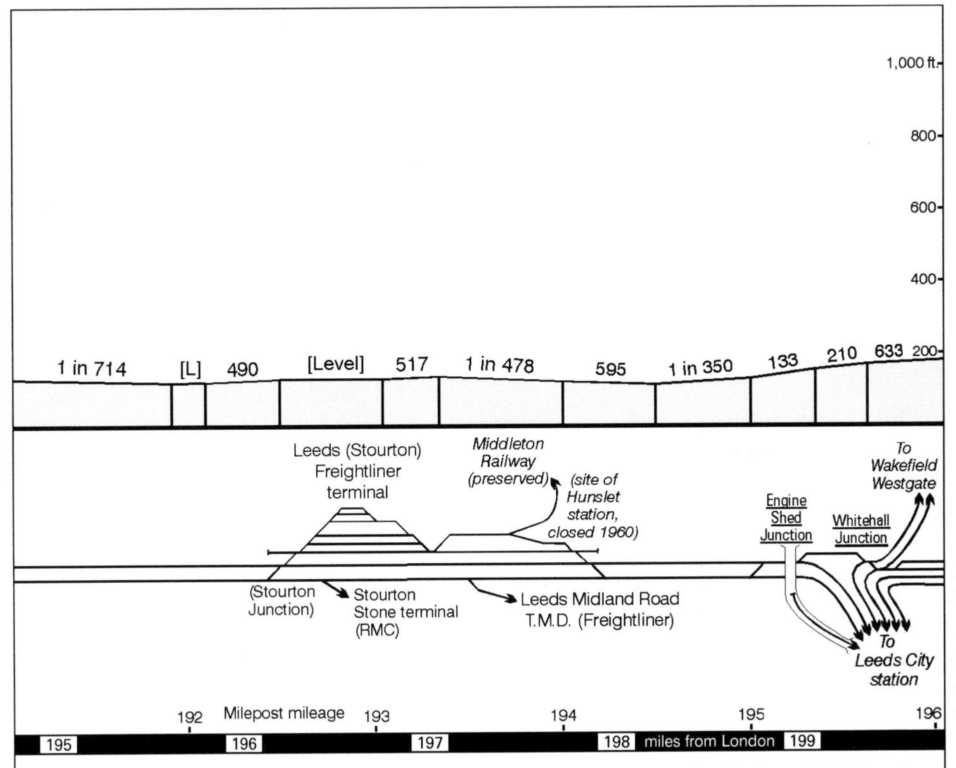

ENGINE SHED JUNCTION : The city of Leeds skyline dominates the background in this view of 66530 heading a rake of Heavy Haul bogie coal empties past Engine Shed Junction. Also visible, the line in the left foreground leads to the former Holbeck shed and the viaduct in the background carrying the ex-LNW line to Huddersfield, albeit now dis-used. (GM 01/03)

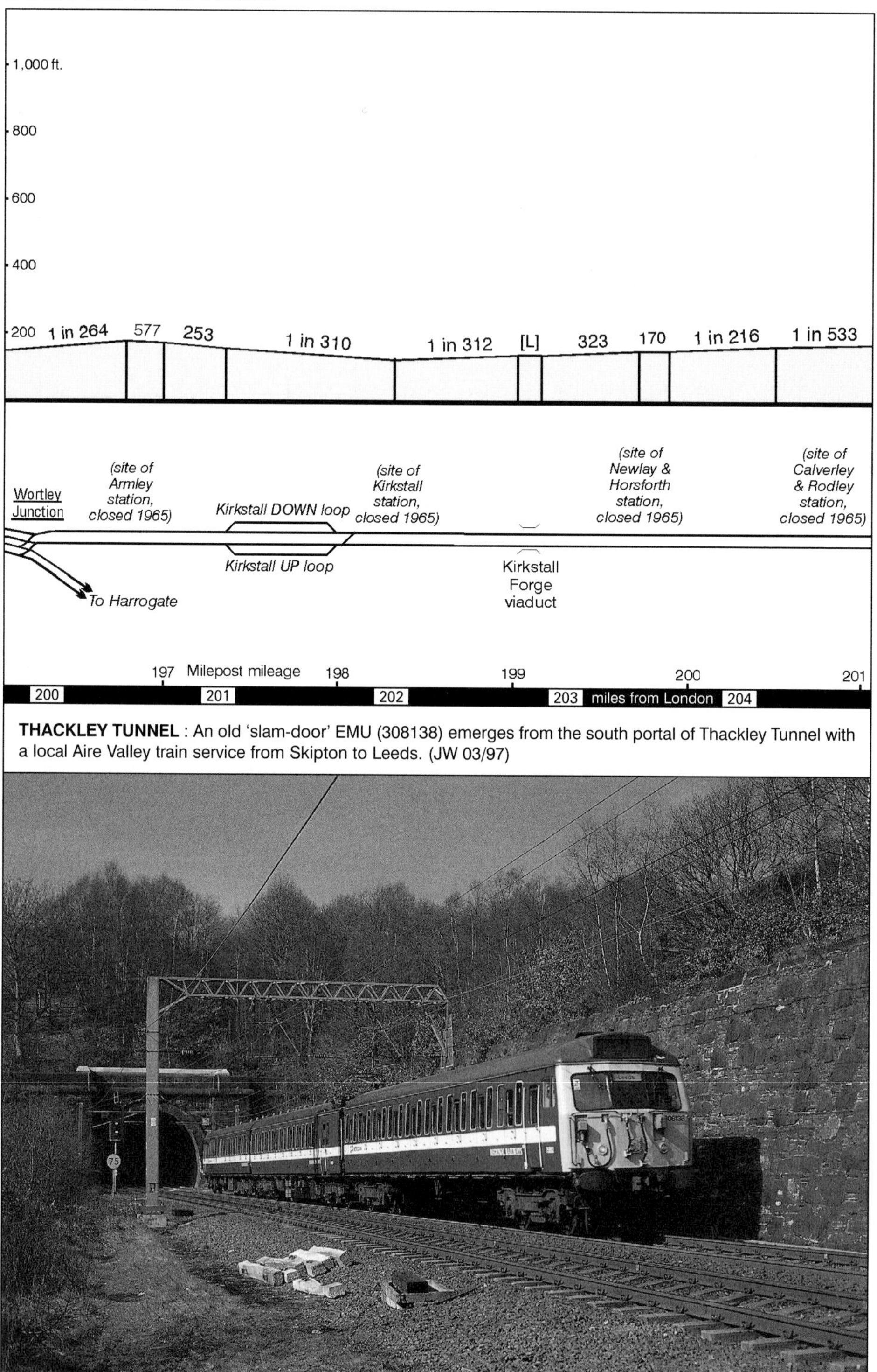

THACKLEY TUNNEL : An old 'slam-door' EMU (308138) emerges from the south portal of Thackley Tunnel with a local Aire Valley train service from Skipton to Leeds. (JW 03/97)

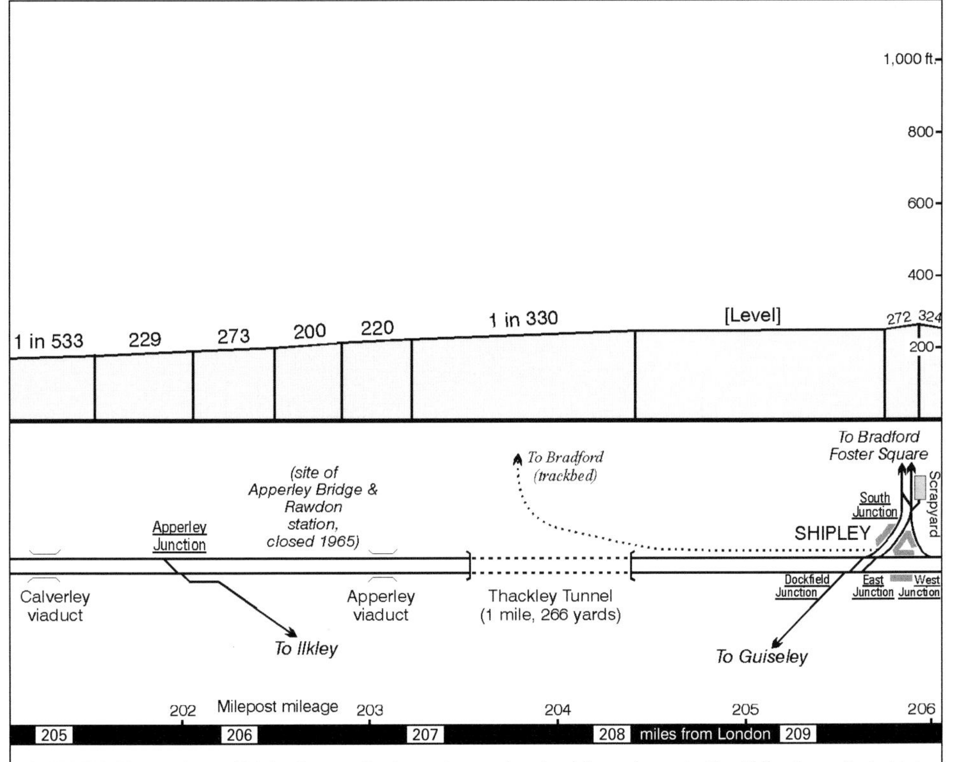

SHIPLEY : The station at Shipley is actually situated on a triangle of lines: the main Aire Valley line, off of which two separate lines give access to/from Bradford Forster Square. Here, 156448 has left Shipley station on the main line and is approaching Shipley West Junction, where the line from Shipley South Junction can be seen trailing in from the right. (GM 09/02)

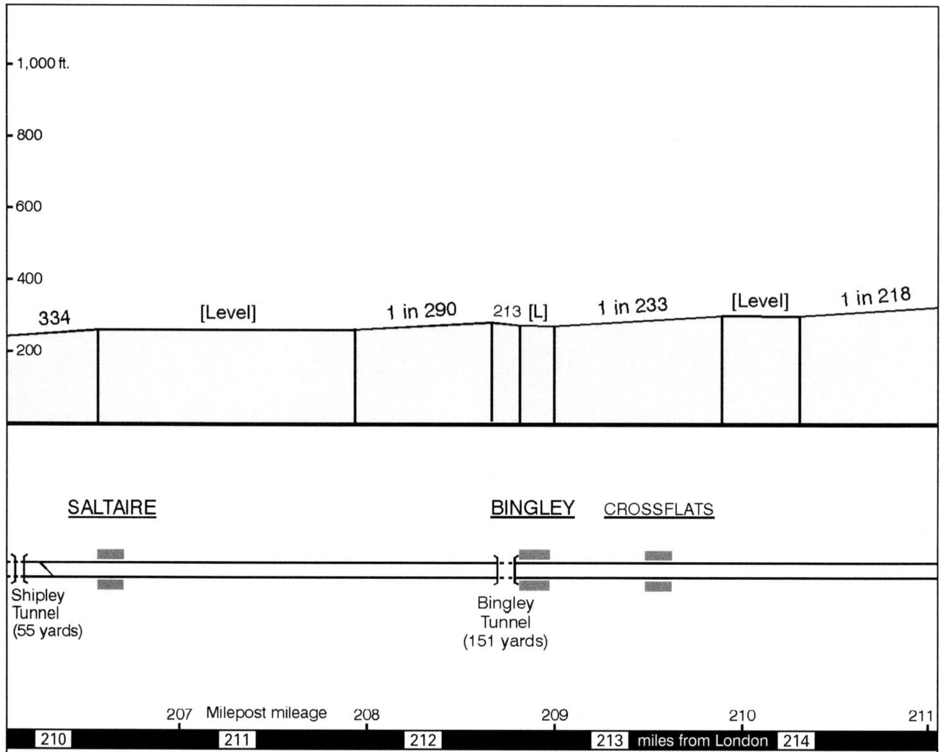

SALTAIRE : A regular passenger service operates between Leeds/Bradford Forster Square and Skipton serving the small stations situated along the Aire Valley route. One such service is seen here at Saltaire in the shape of 'Sprinter' unit 156475, deputising on this occasion for a class 333 electric unit, on the 1312 Bradford Forster Square - Skipton. Of note in the background is the distinctive style of architecture for the many woollen mills which can be seen in this part of the world. (GM 09/02)

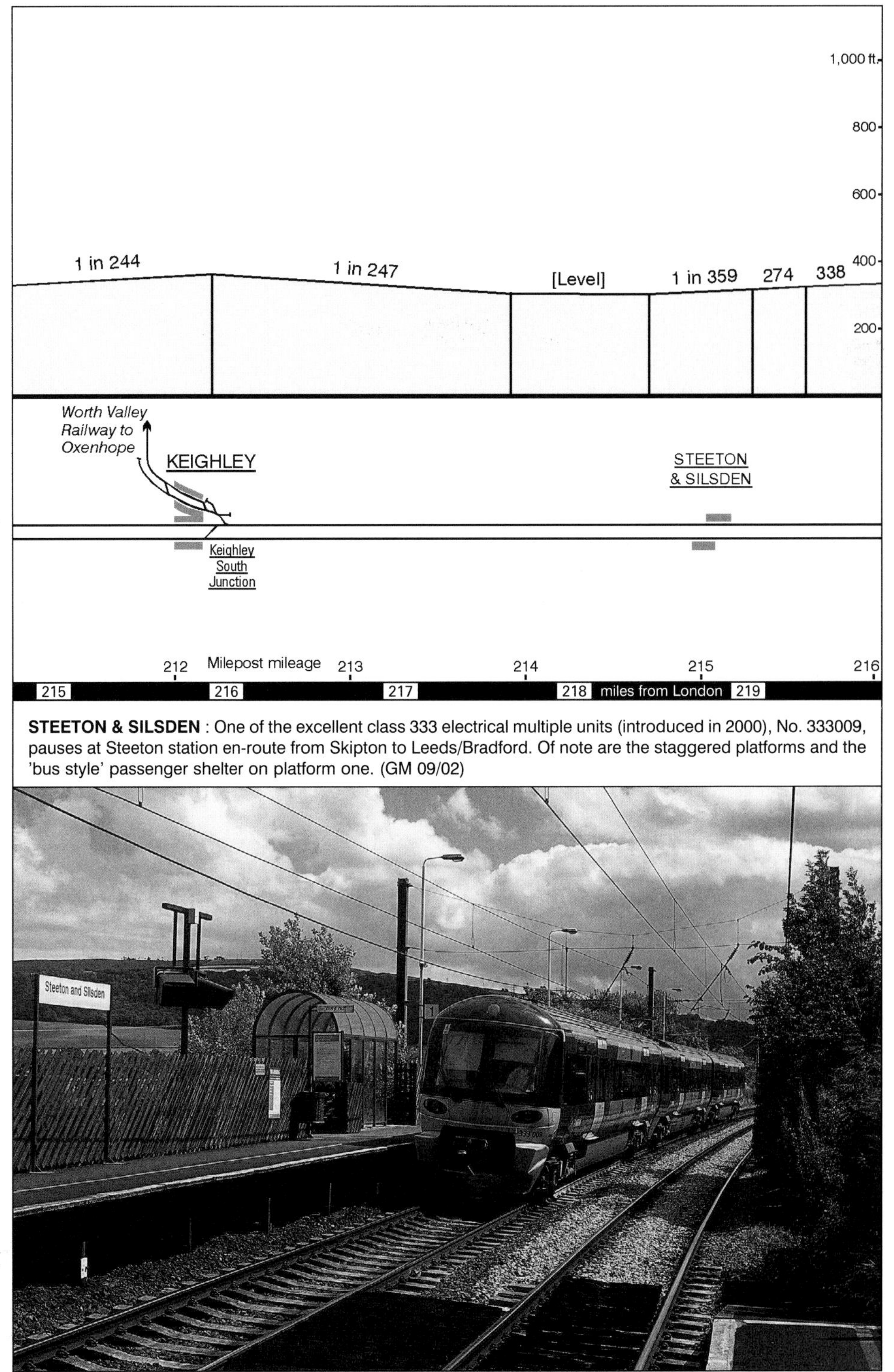

STEETON & SILSDEN : One of the excellent class 333 electrical multiple units (introduced in 2000), No. 333009, pauses at Steeton station en-route from Skipton to Leeds/Bradford. Of note are the staggered platforms and the 'bus style' passenger shelter on platform one. (GM 09/02)

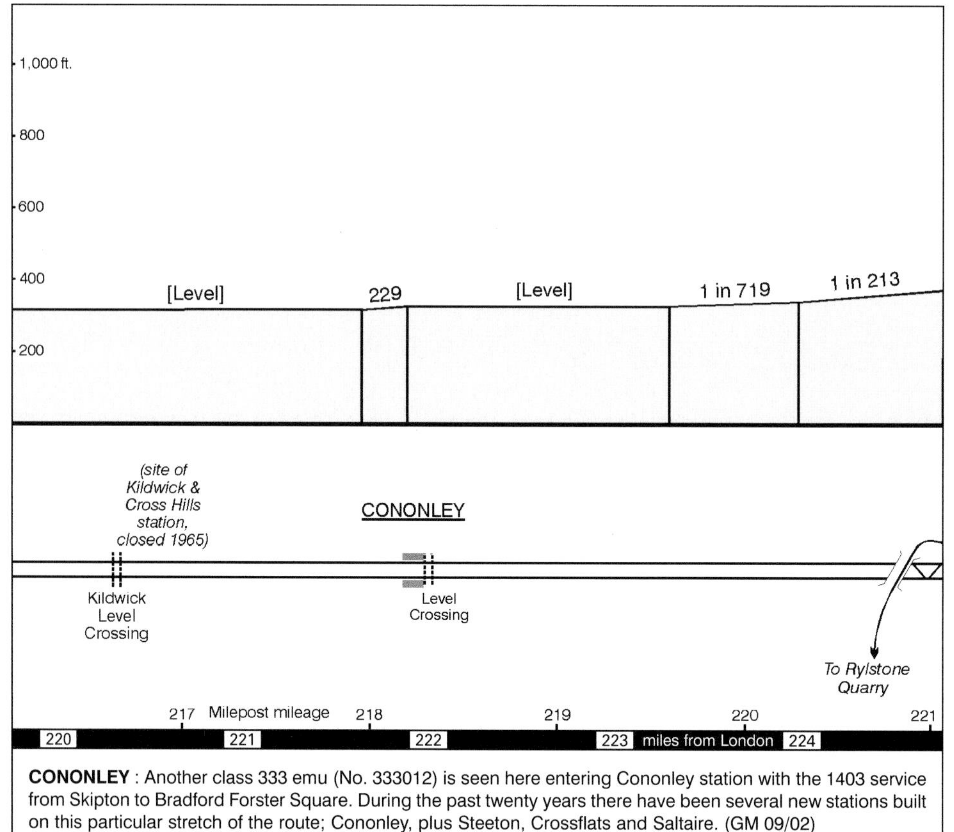

CONONLEY : Another class 333 emu (No. 333012) is seen here entering Cononley station with the 1403 service from Skipton to Bradford Forster Square. During the past twenty years there have been several new stations built on this particular stretch of the route; Cononley, plus Steeton, Crossflats and Saltaire. (GM 09/02)

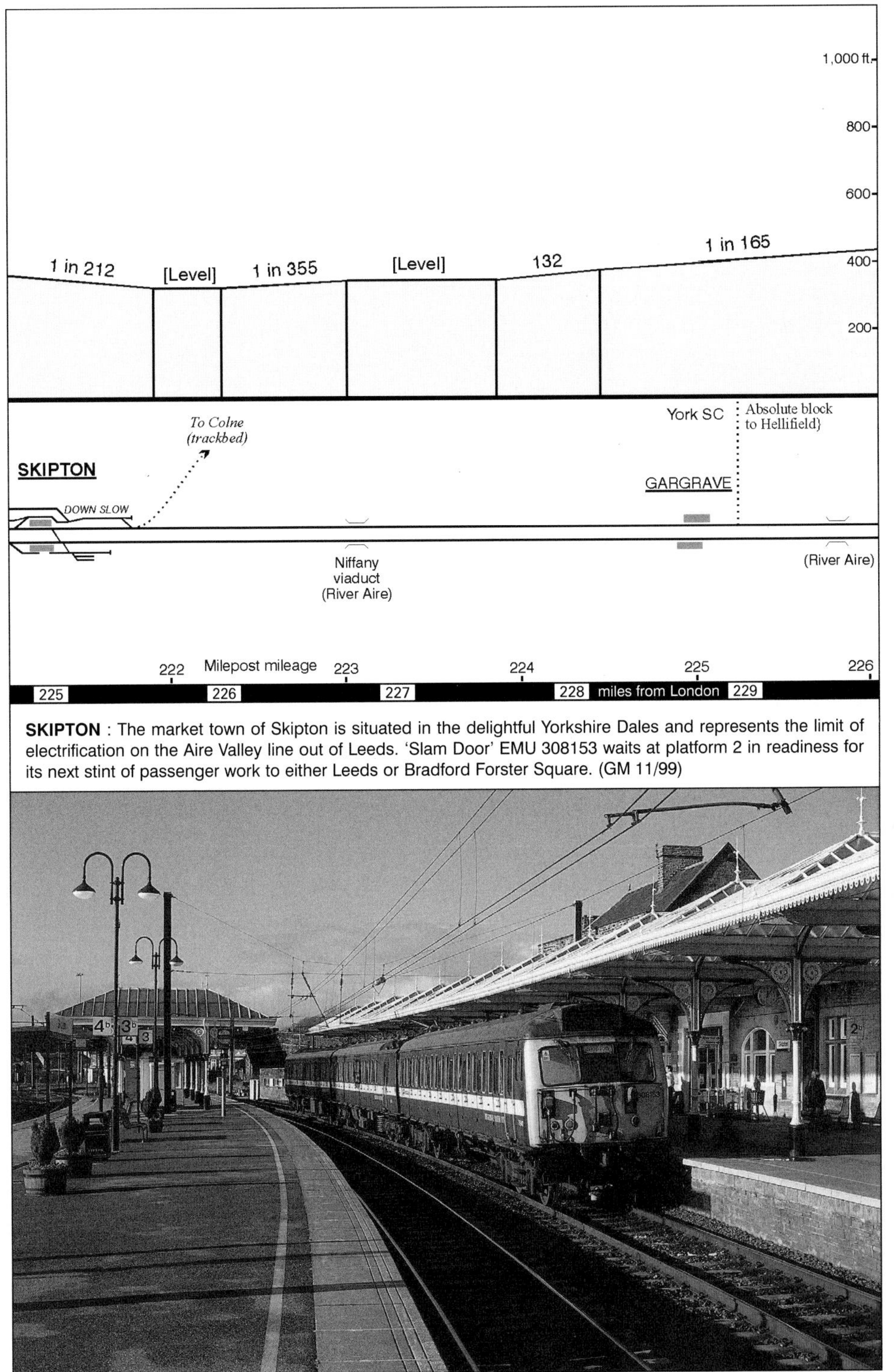

SKIPTON : The market town of Skipton is situated in the delightful Yorkshire Dales and represents the limit of electrification on the Aire Valley line out of Leeds. 'Slam Door' EMU 308153 waits at platform 2 in readiness for its next stint of passenger work to either Leeds or Bradford Forster Square. (GM 11/99)

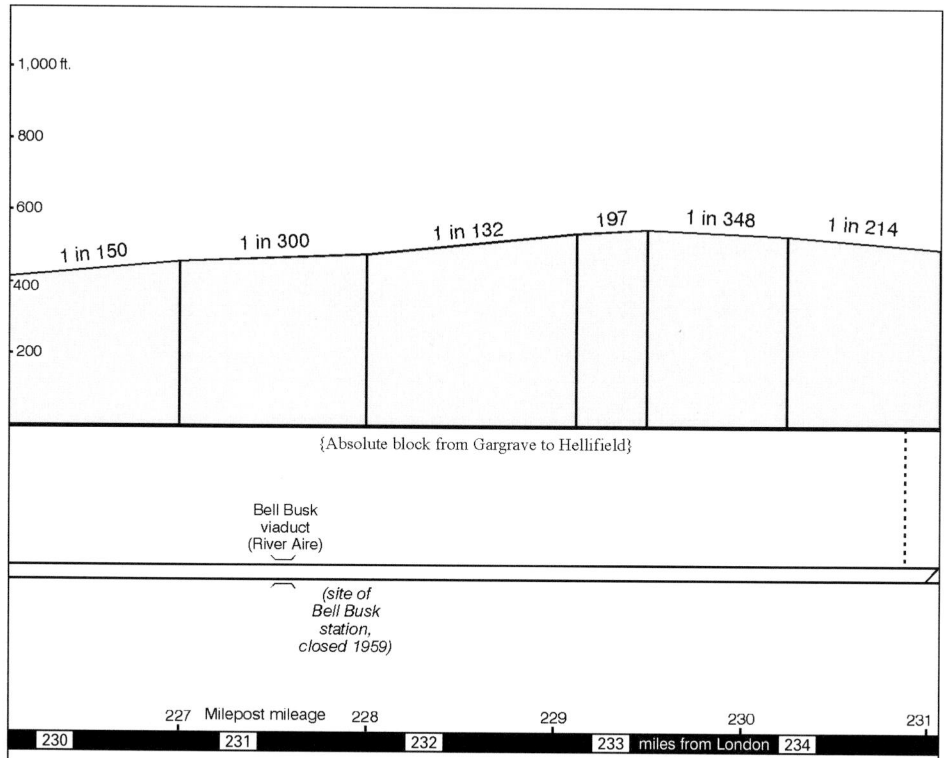

HELLIFIELD : After Skipton, the route leaves the major conurbations behind and passes through some of the most beautiful scenery in the UK, until Carlisle is reached some 87 miles later. Along the way, there are still some good examples of Midland Railway architecture to be seen, such as the station buildings at Settle and Hellifield. The latter is illustrated here and the view is 'train-less' in order to show off the building to good effect - it's a shame the west-end of the platforms have not been maintained to the same high standard! (MB 03/03)

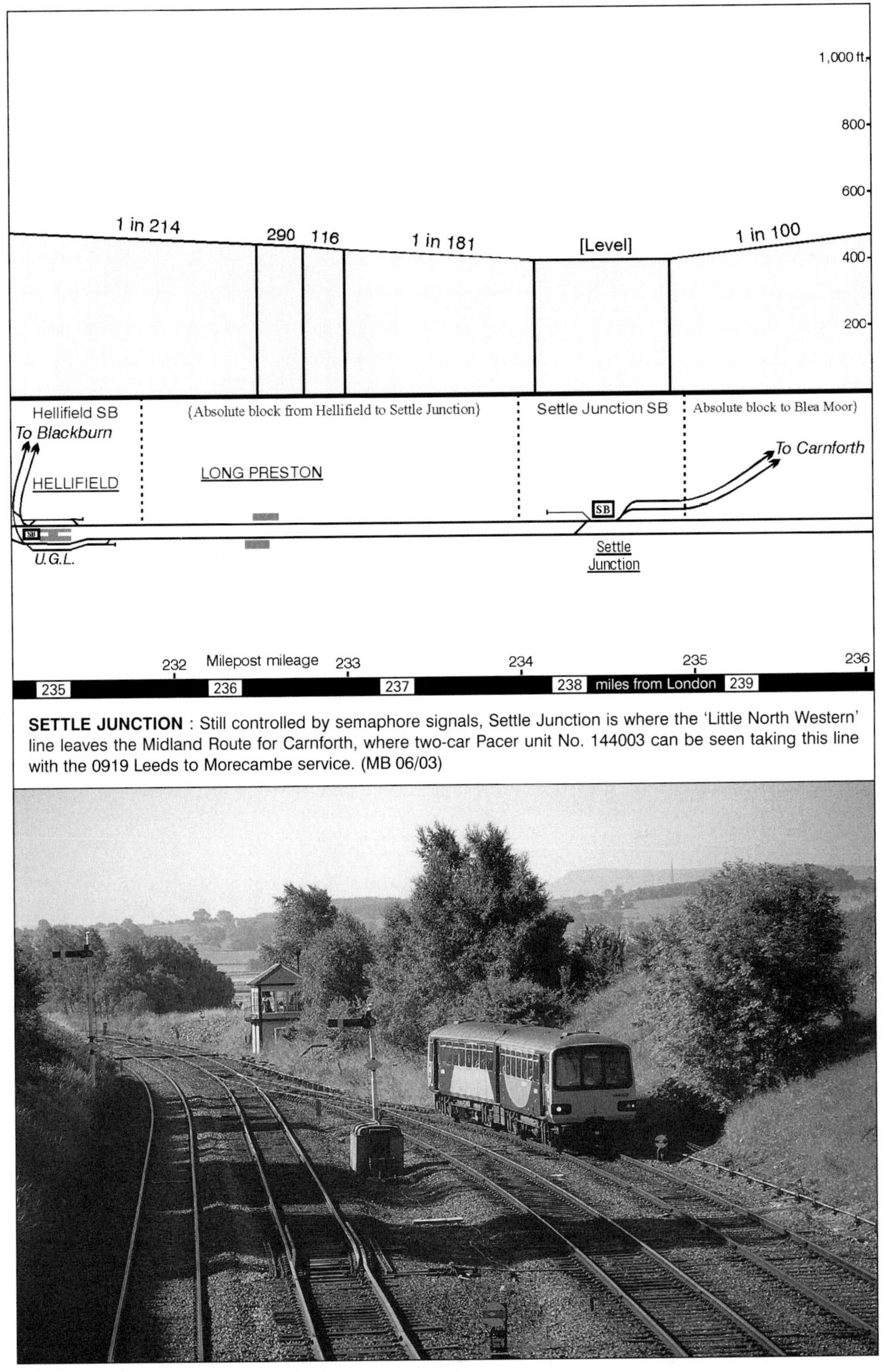

SETTLE JUNCTION : Still controlled by semaphore signals, Settle Junction is where the 'Little North Western' line leaves the Midland Route for Carnforth, where two-car Pacer unit No. 144003 can be seen taking this line with the 0919 Leeds to Morecambe service. (MB 06/03)

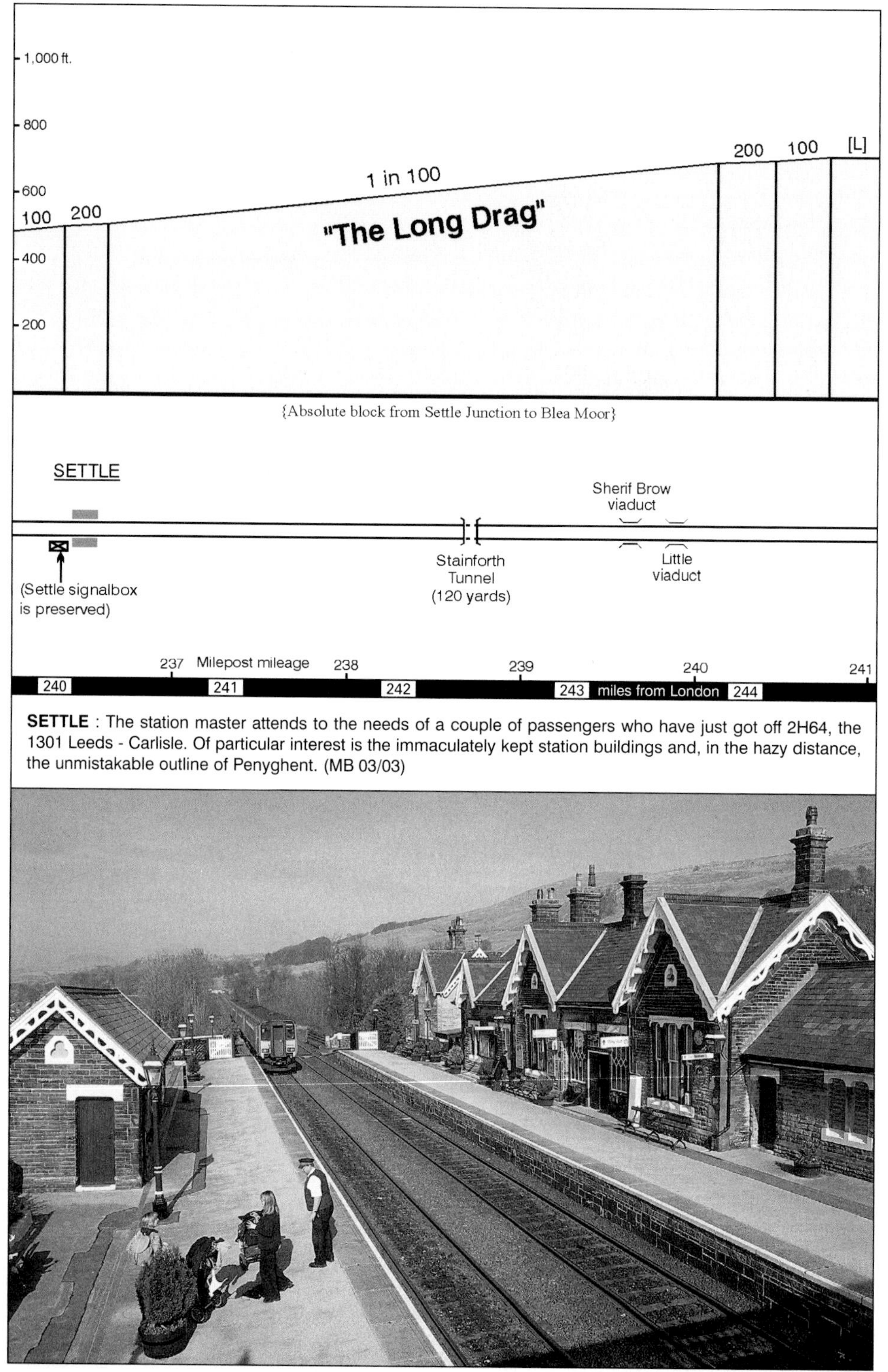

SETTLE : The station master attends to the needs of a couple of passengers who have just got off 2H64, the 1301 Leeds - Carlisle. Of particular interest is the immaculately kept station buildings and, in the hazy distance, the unmistakable outline of Penyghent. (MB 03/03)

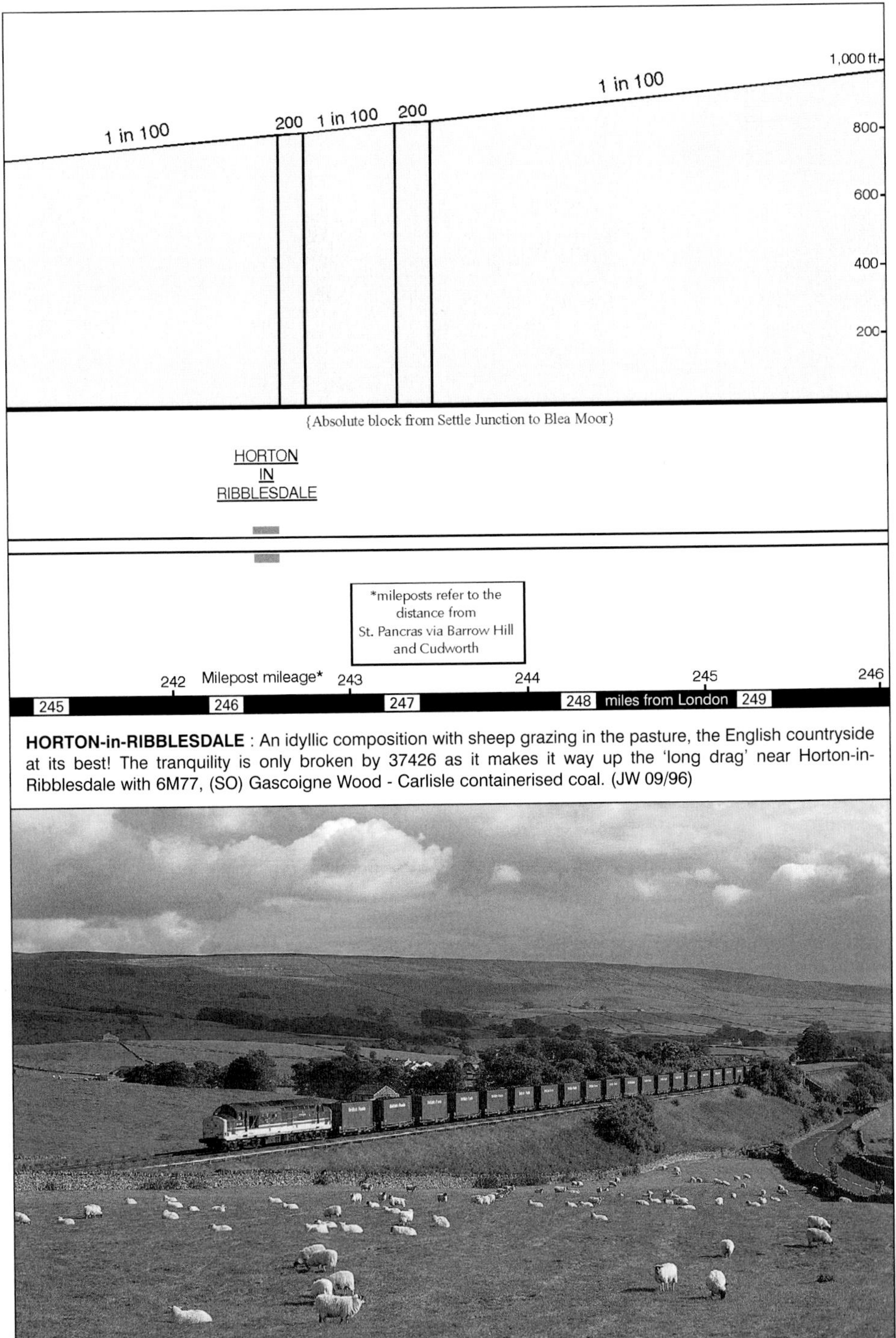

HORTON-in-RIBBLESDALE : An idyllic composition with sheep grazing in the pasture, the English countryside at its best! The tranquility is only broken by 37426 as it makes it way up the 'long drag' near Horton-in-Ribblesdale with 6M77, (SO) Gascoigne Wood - Carlisle containerised coal. (JW 09/96)

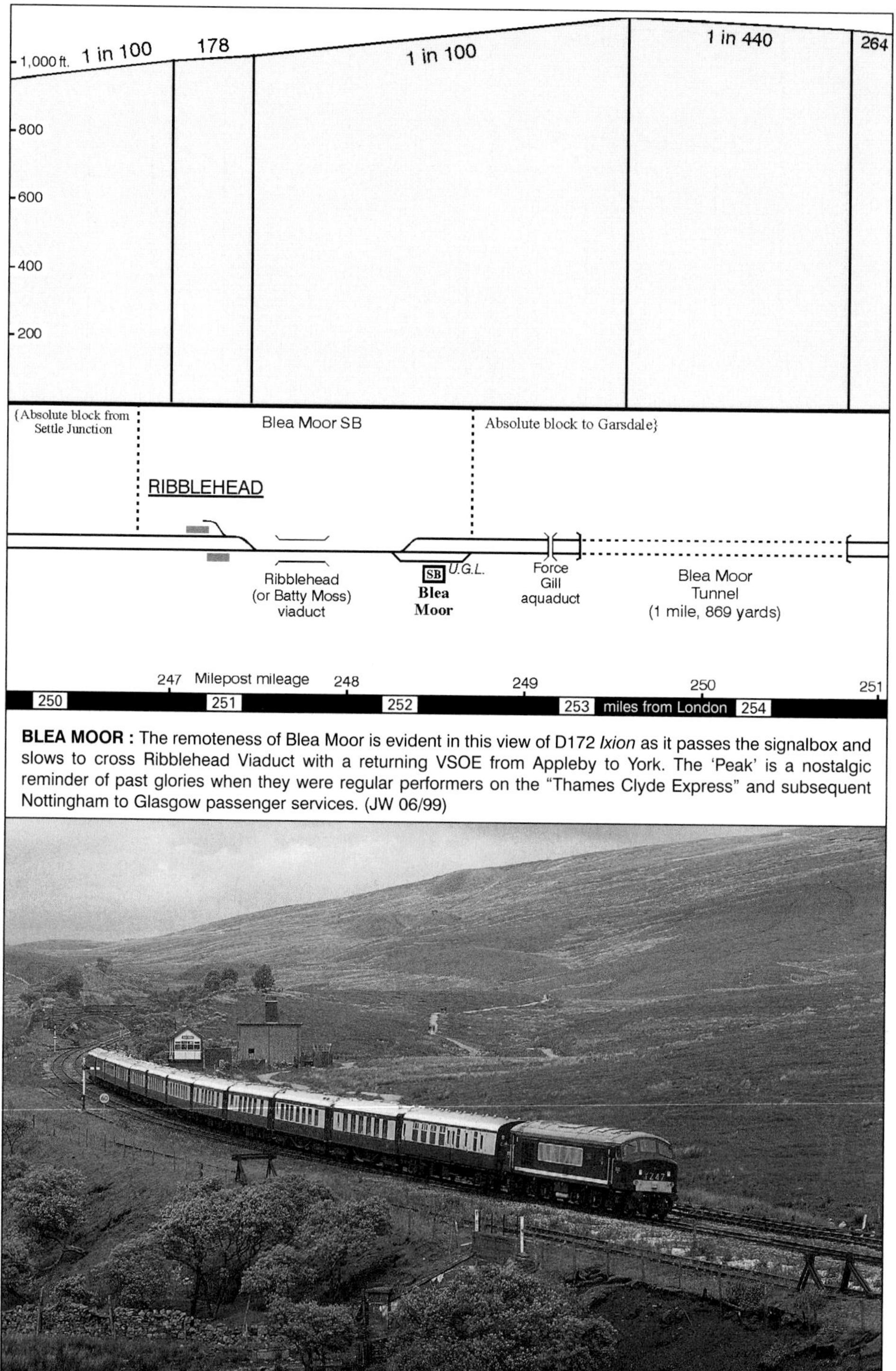

BLEA MOOR : The remoteness of Blea Moor is evident in this view of D172 *Ixion* as it passes the signalbox and slows to cross Ribblehead Viaduct with a returning VSOE from Appleby to York. The 'Peak' is a nostalgic reminder of past glories when they were regular performers on the "Thames Clyde Express" and subsequent Nottingham to Glasgow passenger services. (JW 06/99)

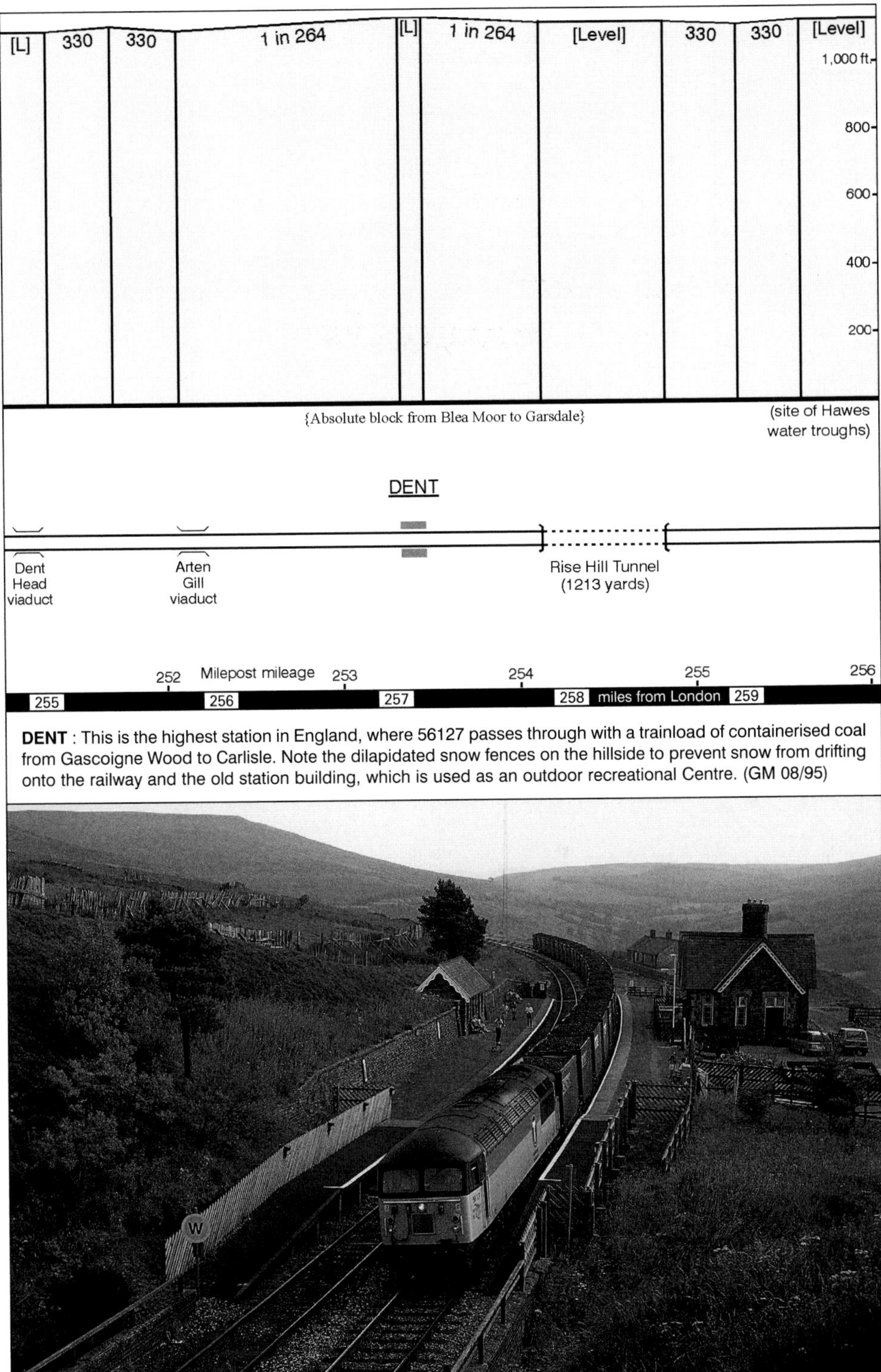

DENT : This is the highest station in England, where 56127 passes through with a trainload of containerised coal from Gascoigne Wood to Carlisle. Note the dilapidated snow fences on the hillside to prevent snow from drifting onto the railway and the old station building, which is used as an outdoor recreational Centre. (GM 08/95)

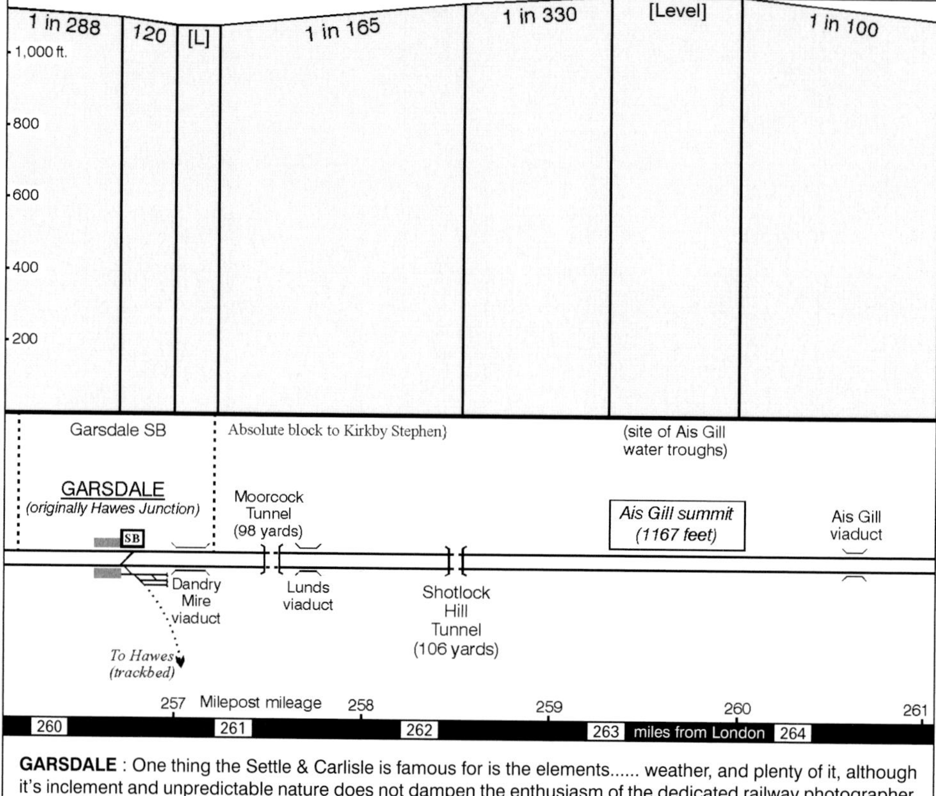

GARSDALE : One thing the Settle & Carlisle is famous for is the elements...... weather, and plenty of it, although it's inclement and unpredictable nature does not dampen the enthusiasm of the dedicated railway photographer. As can be seen from the headcode, D9000 Royal Scots Grey carries the correct reporting for the diverted 0910 (Sat) Edinburgh - Bournemouth as it hurries through Garsdale in driving snow. (DM 03/99)

LUNDS : The S. & C. is an important diversionary route, when engineering work takes passenger services off the West Coast Main Line as can be seen in this panoramic view of 47839 crossing Lunds Viaduct with 1S55, the diverted 0725 Euston - Glasgow Central. Also visible is the northern portal of Moorcock Tunnel and the embankment which carried the former branch line from Garsdale to Hawes. (JW 03/99)

AIS GILL : Whilst the S. & C. has no 'booked' nuclear flask traffic, occasionally trains run between Carlisle/Sellafield and Doncaster for wagon maintenance. One such working is pictured here, returning from Doncaster, on the descent from Ais Gill summit with 20305 hauling a single flask. (RA 05/00)

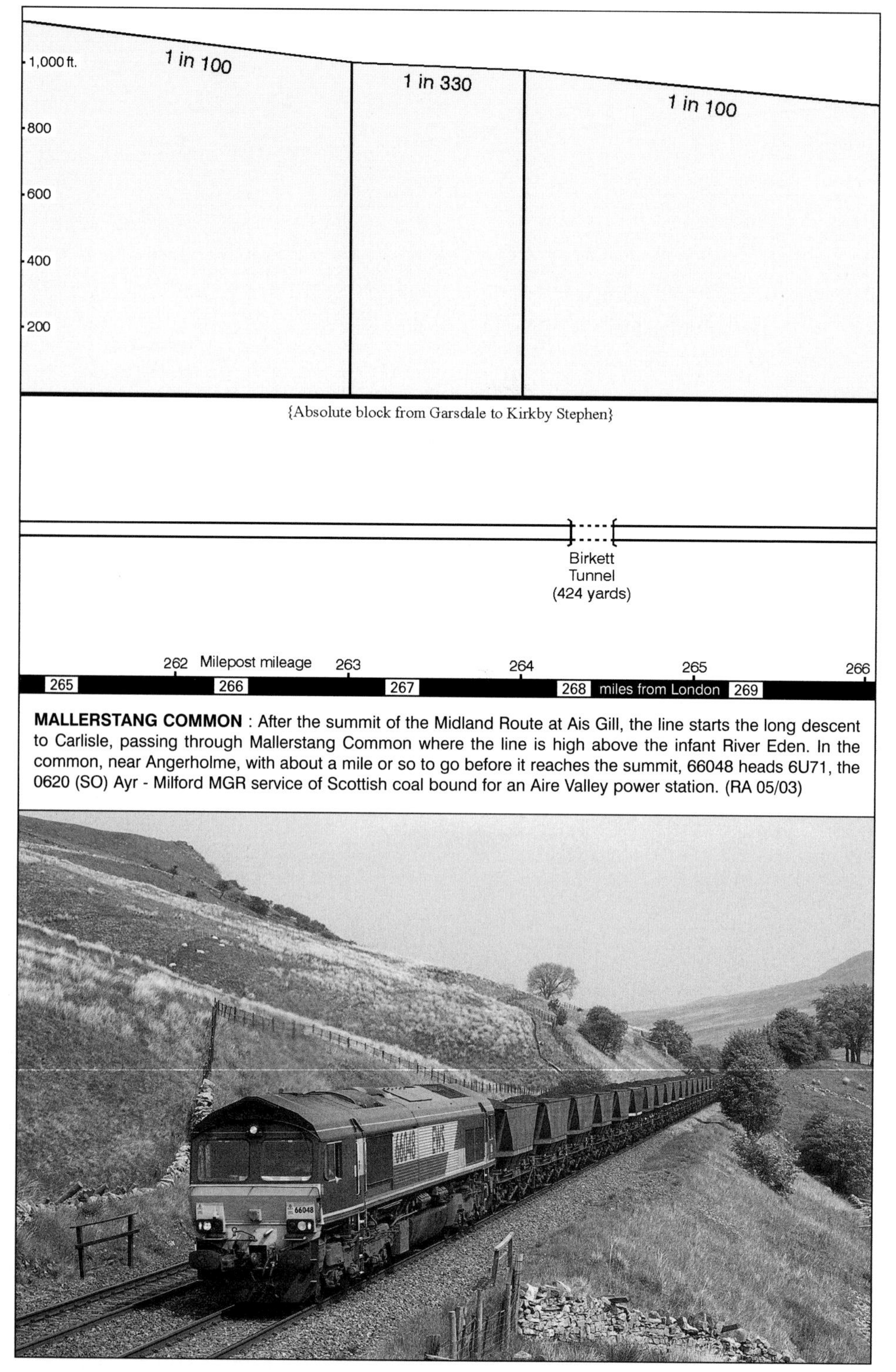

MALLERSTANG COMMON : After the summit of the Midland Route at Ais Gill, the line starts the long descent to Carlisle, passing through Mallerstang Common where the line is high above the infant River Eden. In the common, near Angerholme, with about a mile or so to go before it reaches the summit, 66048 heads 6U71, the 0620 (SO) Ayr - Milford MGR service of Scottish coal bound for an Aire Valley power station. (RA 05/03)

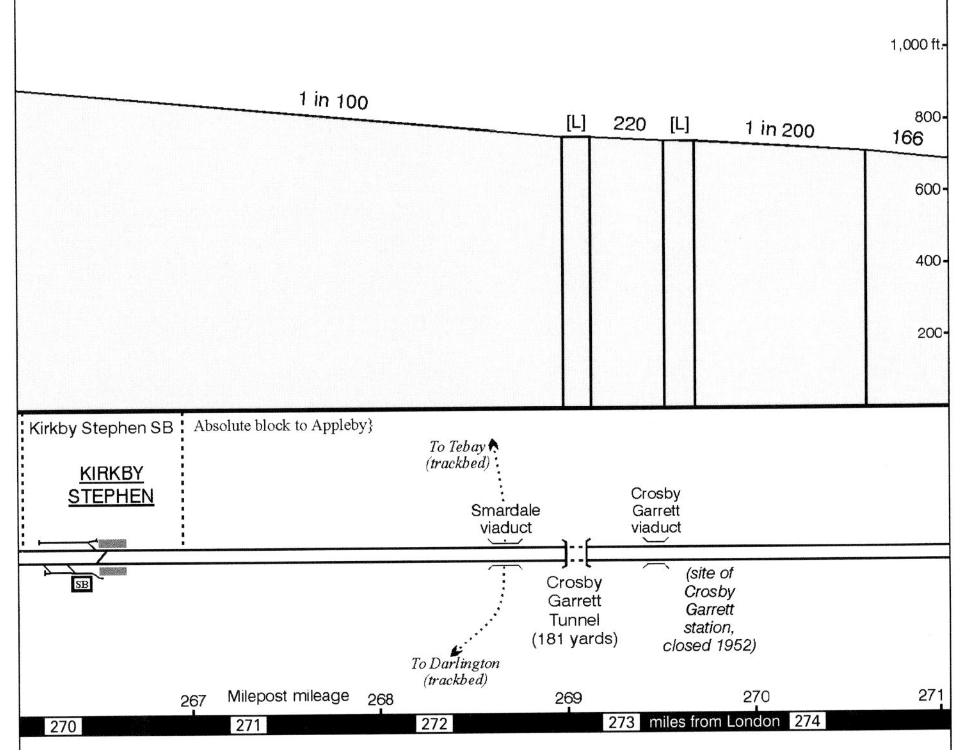

KIRKBY STEPHEN : The station is actually situated some two miles from the market town of Kirkby Stephen, but provides a delightful setting for this view of 66134 passing through the station with 6E13, Newbigginn - Knottingley empty gypsum containers. (RA 04/01)

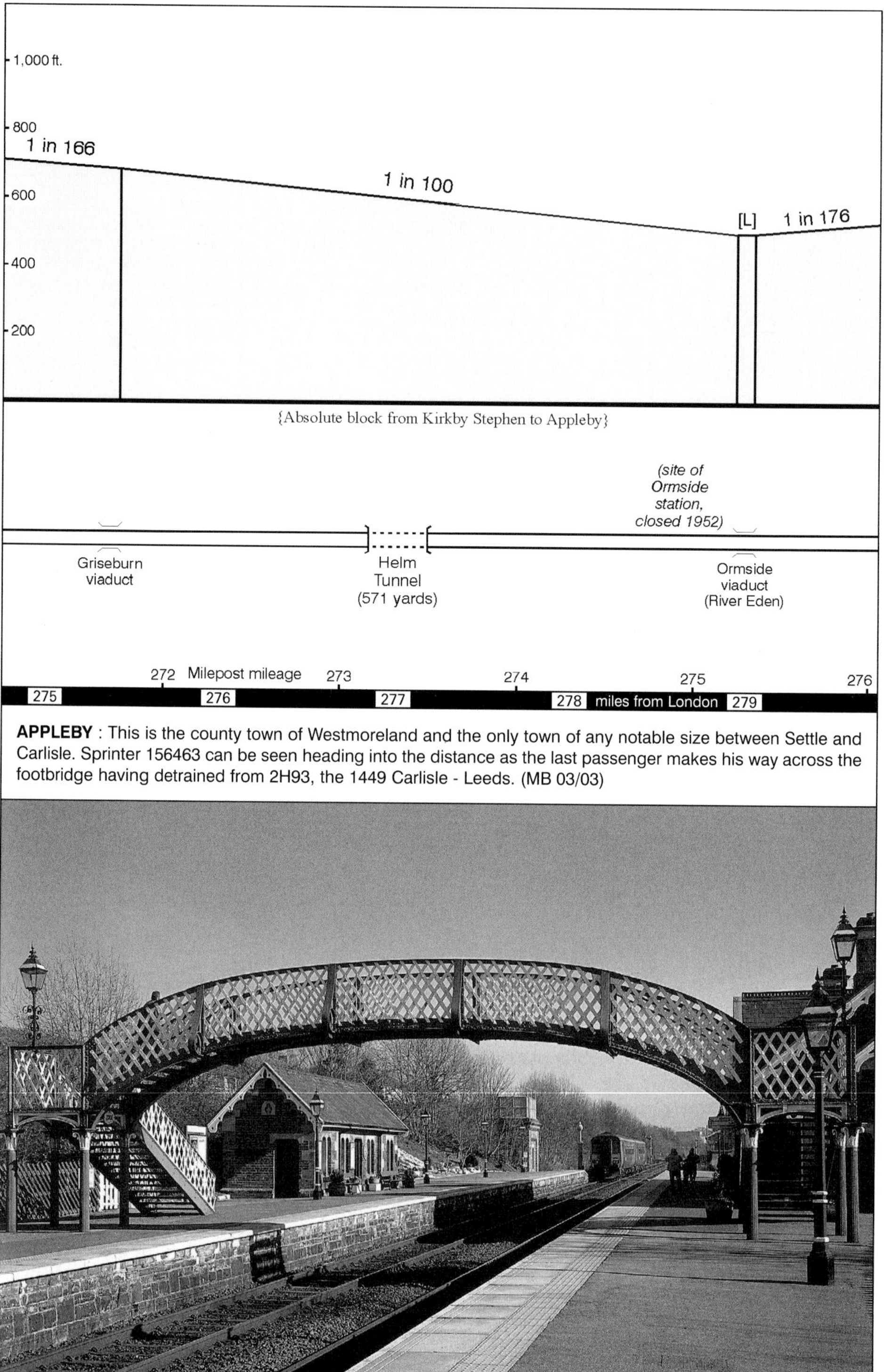

APPLEBY : This is the county town of Westmoreland and the only town of any notable size between Settle and Carlisle. Sprinter 156463 can be seen heading into the distance as the last passenger makes his way across the footbridge having detrained from 2H93, the 1449 Carlisle - Leeds. (MB 03/03)

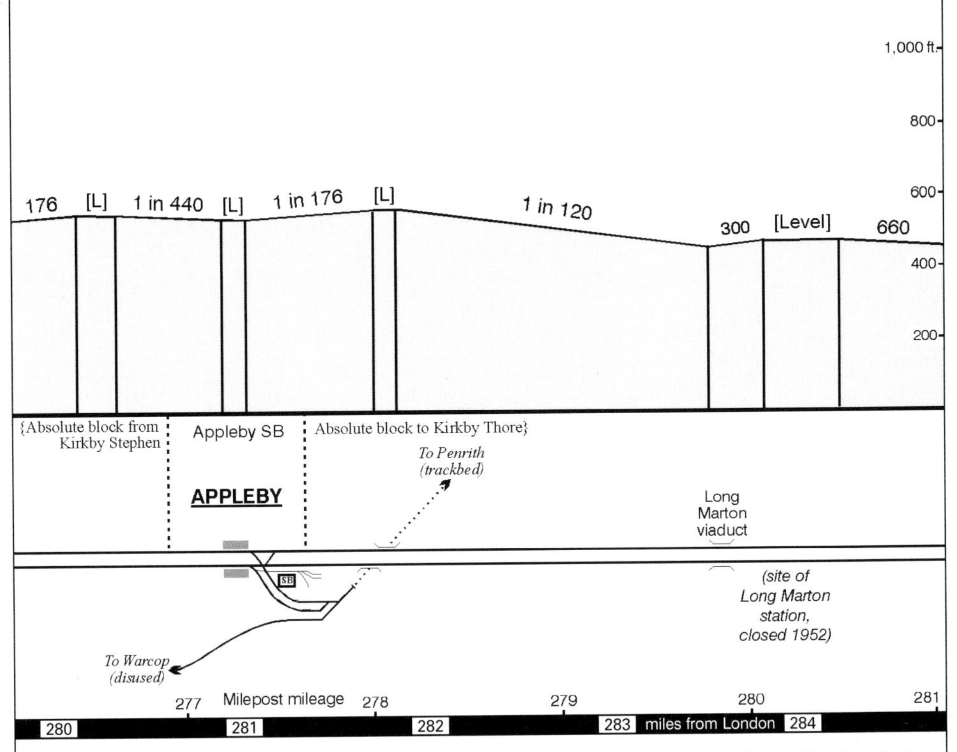

APPLEBY NORTH : This view shows the track layout at the north end of Appleby station along with a fine display of semaphore signals, which are controlled by the signalbox on the 'up' side of the main line. A class 158 unit (158908) on 1E23, the 1410 Glasgow Central - Leeds, passes over the junction which gives access to a spur leading to the disused Warcop branch. (MB 03/03)

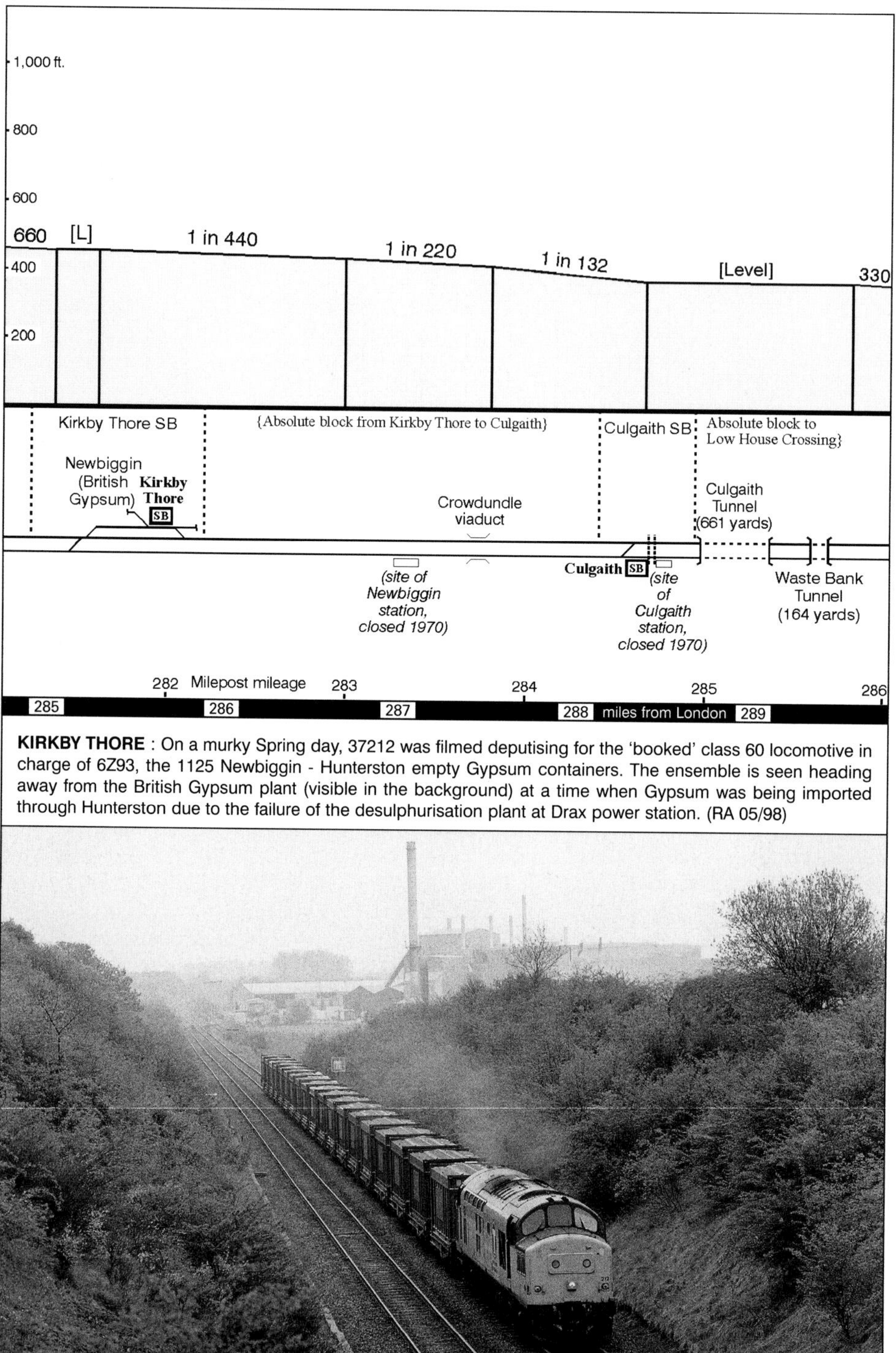

KIRKBY THORE : On a murky Spring day, 37212 was filmed deputising for the 'booked' class 60 locomotive in charge of 6Z93, the 1125 Newbiggin - Hunterston empty Gypsum containers. The ensemble is seen heading away from the British Gypsum plant (visible in the background) at a time when Gypsum was being imported through Hunterston due to the failure of the desulphurisation plant at Drax power station. (RA 05/98)

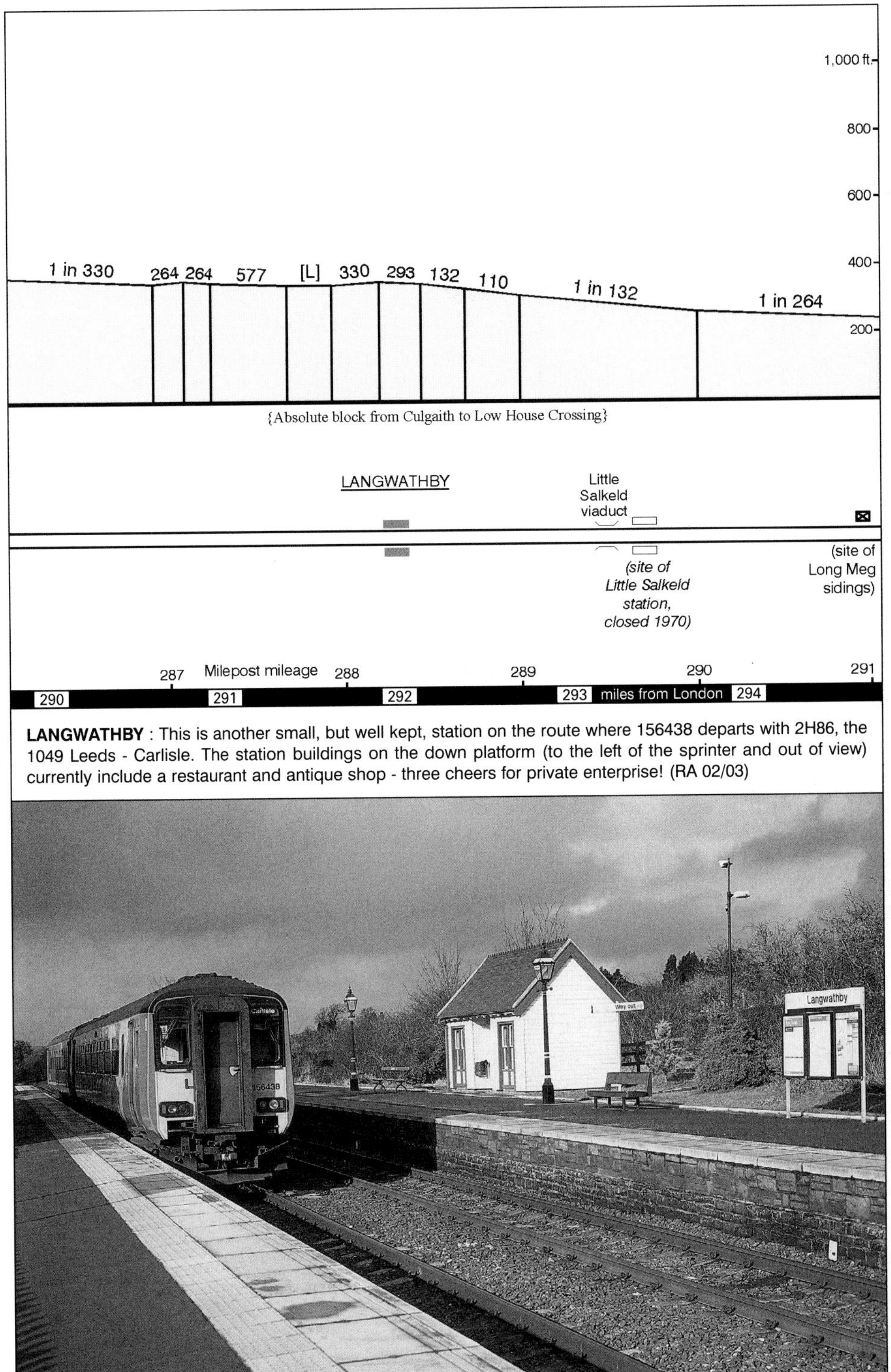

LANGWATHBY : This is another small, but well kept, station on the route where 156438 departs with 2H86, the 1049 Leeds - Carlisle. The station buildings on the down platform (to the left of the sprinter and out of view) currently include a restaurant and antique shop - three cheers for private enterprise! (RA 02/03)

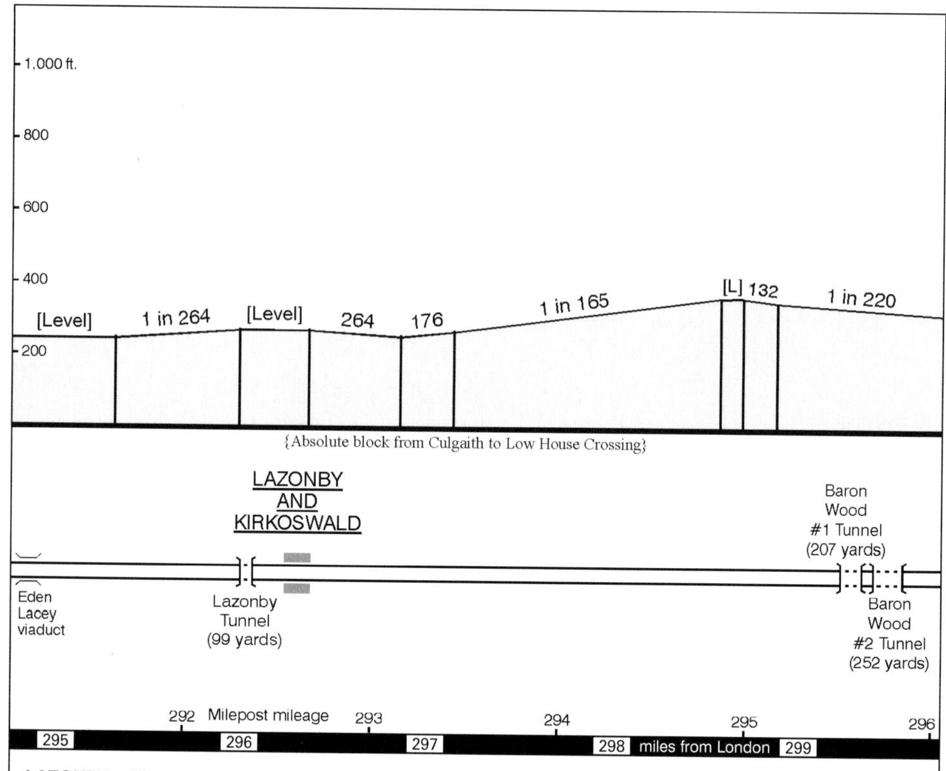

LAZONBY : Pictured a few hundred yards north of Lazonby & Kirkoswald station, 47818 *Strathclyde* heads 1S54, the 0550 (Sun) Bournemouth - Glasgow Central Virgin cross-country service, diverted onto the 'S. & C'. due to engineering work on the WCML. (RA 03/02)

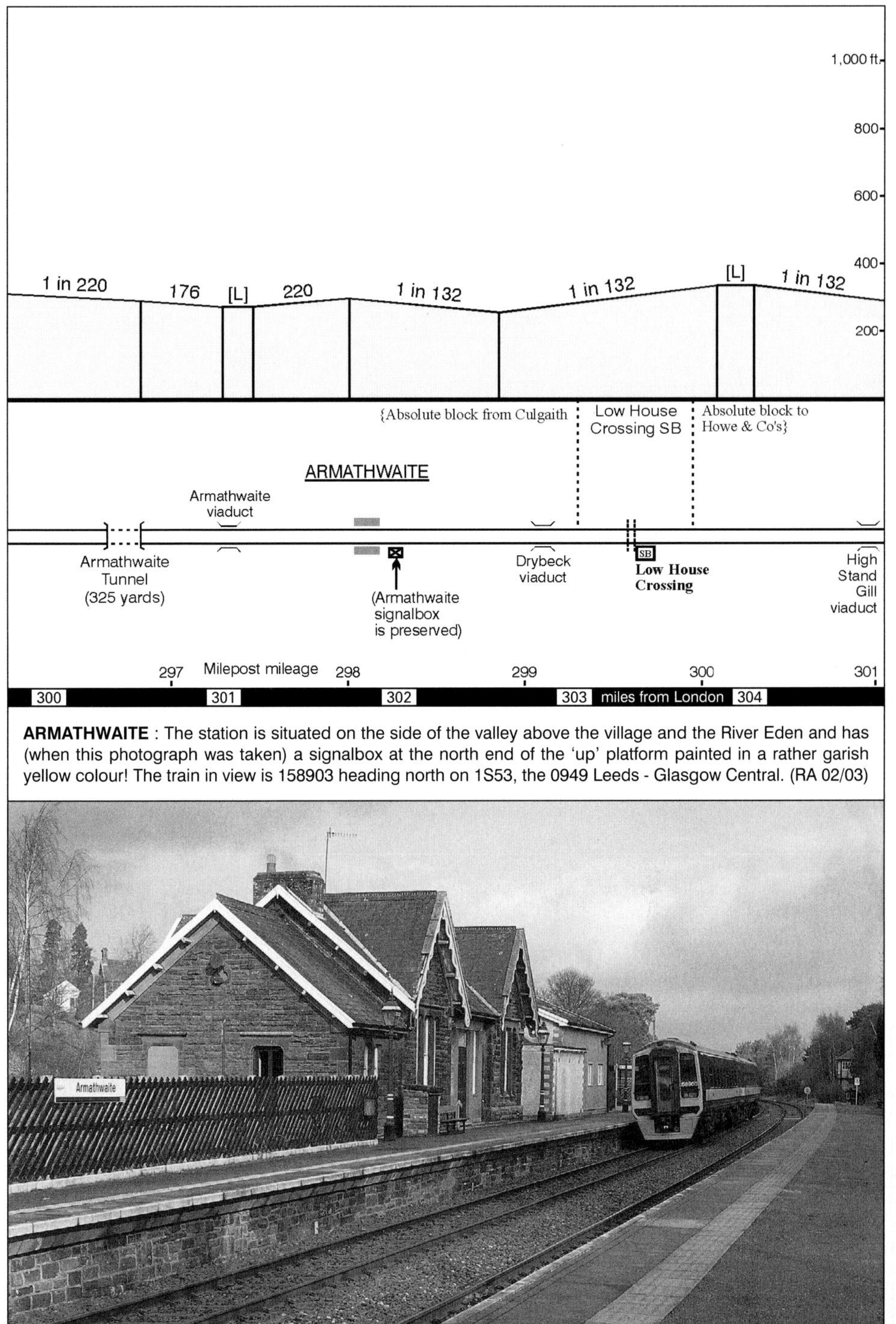

ARMATHWAITE : The station is situated on the side of the valley above the village and the River Eden and has (when this photograph was taken) a signalbox at the north end of the 'up' platform painted in a rather garish yellow colour! The train in view is 158903 heading north on 1S53, the 0949 Leeds - Glasgow Central. (RA 02/03)

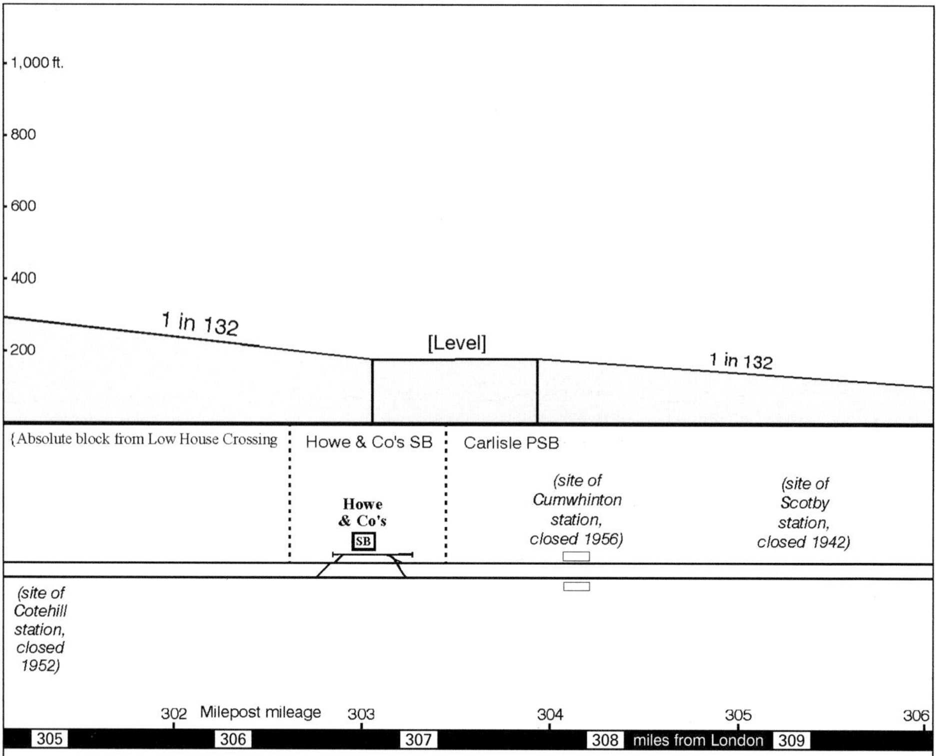

1,000 ft.
800
600
400
200

1 in 132

[Level]

1 in 132

{Absolute block from Low House Crossing

Howe & Co's SB

Carlisle PSB

(site of Cumwhinton station, closed 1956)

(site of Scotby station, closed 1942)

Howe & Co's SB

(site of Cotehill station, closed 1952)

302 Milepost mileage 303 304 305 306

305 306 307 308 miles from London 309

CARLISLE LONDON ROAD : The goods depot at London Road looks in a state of dereliction as156448 passes with the 1325 Newcastle - Carlisle. The coal depot can be seen in the background plus Petteril Bridge Junction, where the Settle & Carlisle diverges to the right. (DM 05/96)

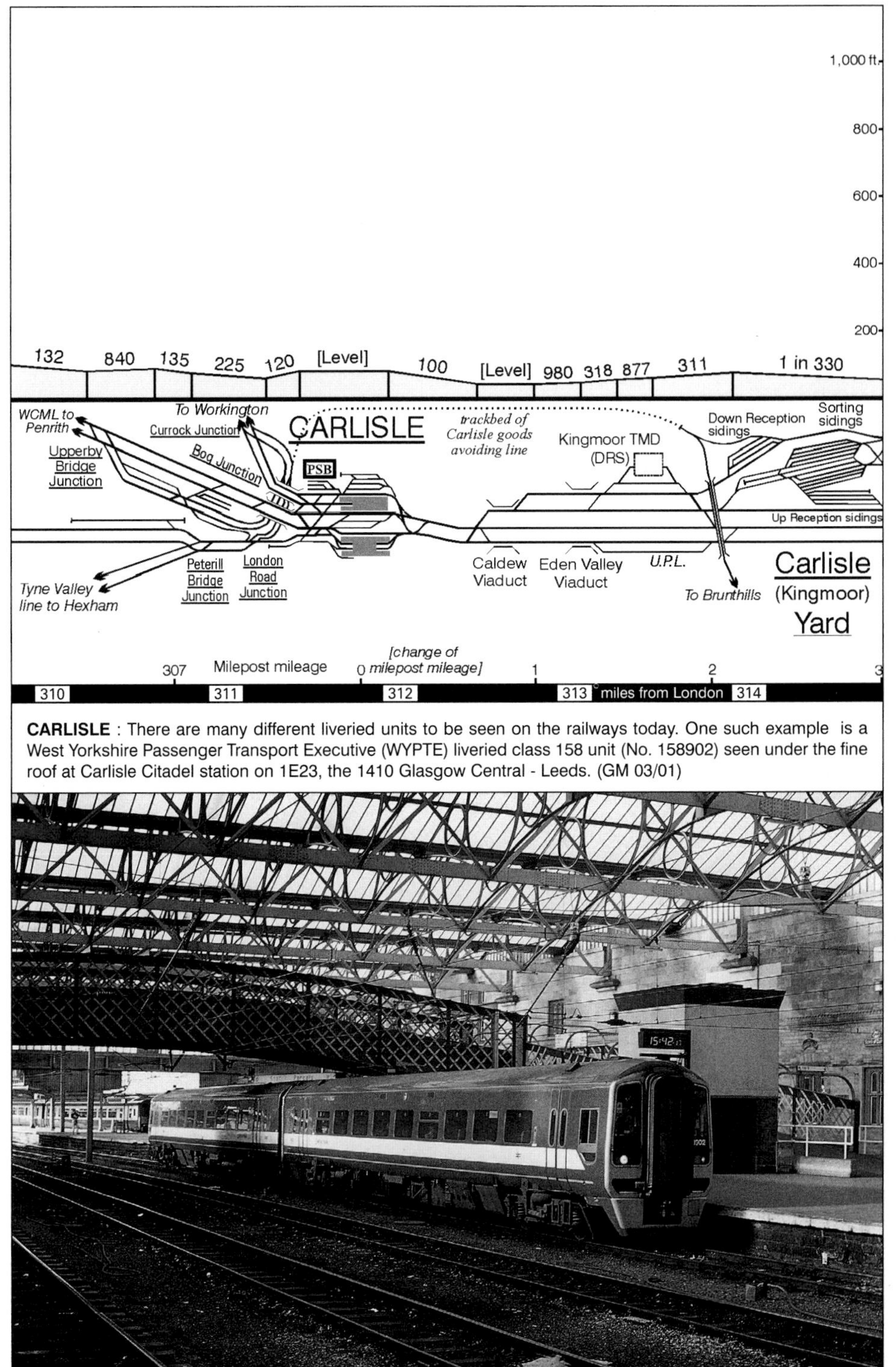

CARLISLE : There are many different liveried units to be seen on the railways today. One such example is a West Yorkshire Passenger Transport Executive (WYPTE) liveried class 158 unit (No. 158902) seen under the fine roof at Carlisle Citadel station on 1E23, the 1410 Glasgow Central - Leeds. (GM 03/01)

CARLISLE YARD : Although the yard is a shadow of its former self, it is still an important centre for freight services, especially 'Enterprise' traffic and coal trains. Substituting for the 'booked' class 92 locomotive, 66007 (*above*) heads a lengthy 6012, Carlisle Yard - Eastleigh 'Enterprise' out of the yard, including MOD traffic in the consist which had been 'tripped' to Carlisle from Eastriggs earlier in the day. (MB 07/03)

Anglo-Scottish coal trains are staged at Carlisle pending paths between the Ayrshire coalfield and English power stations. Here, 66247 and 66067 (*below*) stand at the head of two rakes of empty EWS coal hoppers in readiness for a path to Falkland Junction, Ayr. (MB 07/03)

Gallery

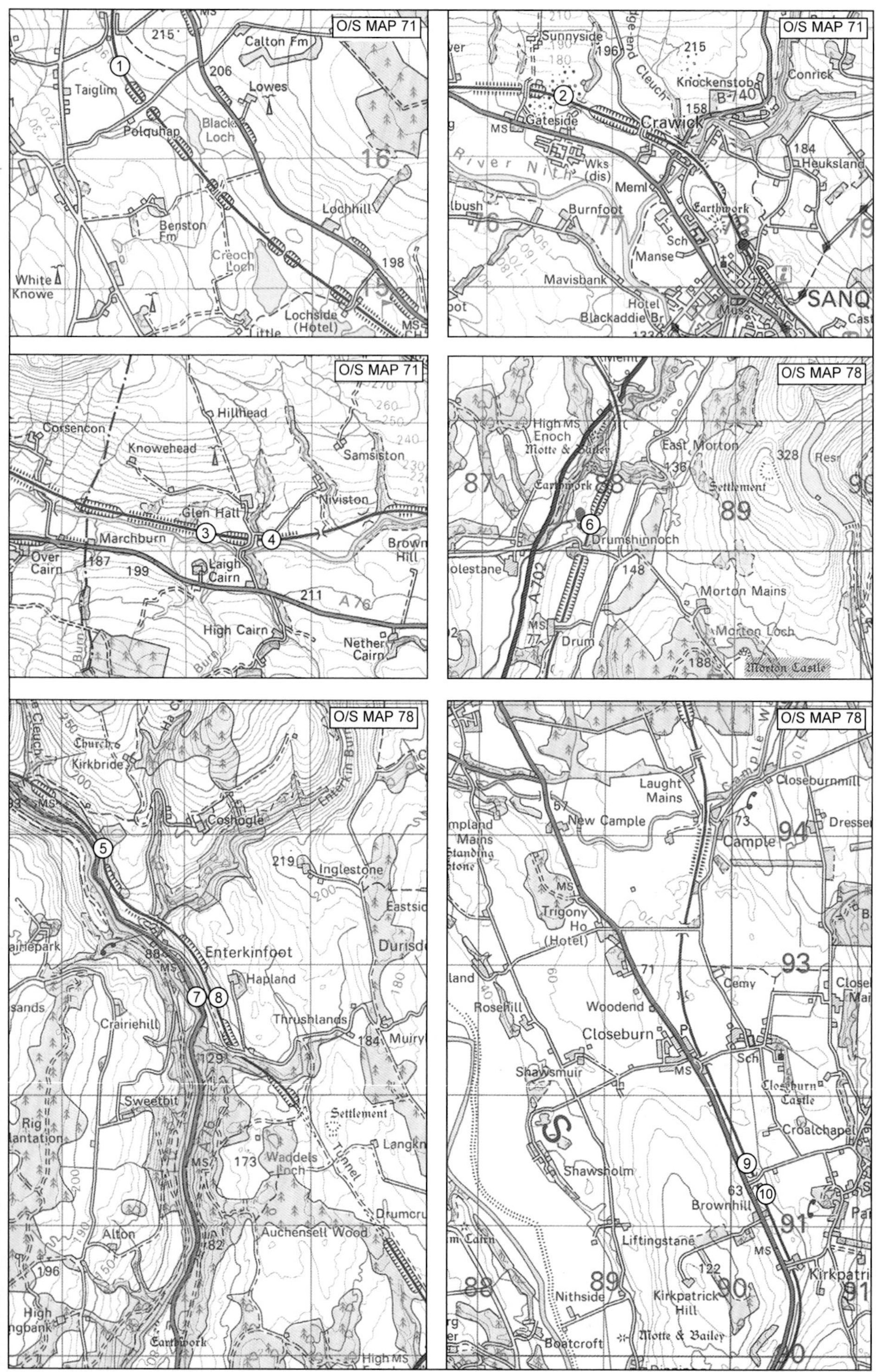
O/S MAP 71
Calton Fm
Taiglim
Lowes
Polquhap
Black Loch
Benston Fm
Creoch Loch
Lochhill
White Knowe
Lochside (Hotel)
Little
O/S MAP 71
Sunnyside
Knockenstob
Conrick
B 740
Gateside
Crawick
River Nith
Wks (dis)
Meml
Heuksland
Burnfoot
Earthwork
Sch
Manse
Mavisbank
Hotel
Blackaddie Br
SANQ
O/S MAP 71
Hillhead
Corsencon
Knowehead
Samsiston
Niviston
Glen Hall
Marchburn
Over Cairn
Laigh Cairn
Brown Hill
A 76
High Cairn
Nether Cairn
O/S MAP 78
High Enoch
Motte & Bailey
East Morton
Earthwork
Settlement
Drumshinnoch
Morton Mains
A 702
Drum
Morton Loch
Morton Castle
O/S MAP 78
Church
Kirkbride
Coshogle
Enterkin Burn
Inglestone
Eastside
Durisdeer
Enterkinfoot
Hapland
Crairiehill
Thrushlands
Muiryhill
Sweetbit
Settlement
Rig Plantation
Waddels Loch
Tunnel
Langknowe
Drumcruilton
Alton
Auchensell Wood
High Ingbank
Earthwork
O/S MAP 78
Closeburnmill
Laught Mains
New Cample
Cample
Dressert
Trigony Ho (Hotel)
Cemy
Woodend
Closeburn
Rosehill
Shawsmuir
Closeburn Castle
Croalchapel
Shawsholm
Brownhill
Liftingstane
Kirkpatrick Hill
Nithside
Motte & Bailey
Boatcroft

① **POLQUHAP** : Polquhap is the highest point on the G & SW between Carlisle and Glasgow and is where the photographer captured 37803+37116 *Sister Dora* working hard hauling a rake of loaded MEA box wagons of coal, forming 6Z38, the 1320 Ayr Falkland Junction - Clitheroe cement works. (RA 05/97)

② **GATESIDE** : Midway between Kirkconnel and Sanquhar, 156501 passes the site of former open cast coal workings at gateside with 1S74, the 1236 Newcastle - Stranraer. The scenery is really beautiful in this region of the Nith Valley where the Lowther Hills provide a dramatic backdrop. (DM 03/00)

(3) **GLEN HALL** : Late Autumn is a delightful time for photography with the colourful turning of the leaves and weakening sunshine as can be seen in this view at Glen Hall of 66524 (*above*) heading east with a 'special' train of coal en-route from New Cumnock to Eggborough power station. (BA 11/01)

(4) Looking in the opposite direction, 60079 *Foinaven* (*below*) heads 6S36, Dalston - Grangemouth empty petroleum tanks, which would normally travel direct from Carlisle via beattock, but diverted via the G &SW on this particular occasion. (PJR 10/99)

⑤ **KIRKBRIDE** : Just north of the well known photographic 'hotspot' at Enterkinfoot, the line hugs the hillside near Kirkbride, high above the A76 road and the wooded valley of the River Nith. At this point, we see 66121 heading north with MGR empties bound for Ayr, Falkland Junction. This photograph has been published before, but no apology is made for doing so again! (DM 05/00)

⑥ **DRUMSHINNOCK** : Freight traffic on the old G & SW section of the Midland Route via Dumfries is ostensibly MGR coal traffic emanating from the Ayrshire coalfield and one such service is captured on film in this view taken near Drumshinnock. These days, the ubiquitous 'shed' is 'booked' to work these trains and 66004 was the train engine when this picture was taken. (DM 03/00)

⑦ **ENTERKINFOOT** : Two views of thispopular location are included to show how the vista changes with the seasons. In this view in early Spring, there are decidedly light and subdued colours as 156477 (*above*) passes Enterkinfoot forming 1M88, the 1203 Glasgow Central - Carlisle. About 300 yards further on, the train will enter the north portal of Drumlanrig Tunnel. (MB 03/03)

⑧ In Summer, the view has completely changed and there is a vibrancy of colour. Winding its way up to a mini summit at Drumlanrig, 66215 (*below*) heads 6M32, the 1138 Ayr Falkland Junction - Crewe South Yard, where the train will be staged before leaving for either Ironbridge or Rugelely power station. (MB 07/03)

(9) **CLOSEBURN** : Just south of Closeburn, at Brownhill to be precise, we see yet another 66-hauled load of coal, albeit this time the consist is a rake of grubby looking EWS bogie coal hoppers. 66018 (*above*) heads south with 6E24, the 0620 (TO) Ayr Falkland Yard - Ferrybridge power station. (MB 07/03)

(10) Looking in the opposite direction towards open farmland, 37608+37610 (*below*) head MGR empties forming 6S14, the 0520 Bescot - Ayr Falkland Junction. This was a time when EWS hired in DRS locomotives to work MGR services between Ayr and Carlisle, providing a bonus for railway photographers! (PJR 03/00)

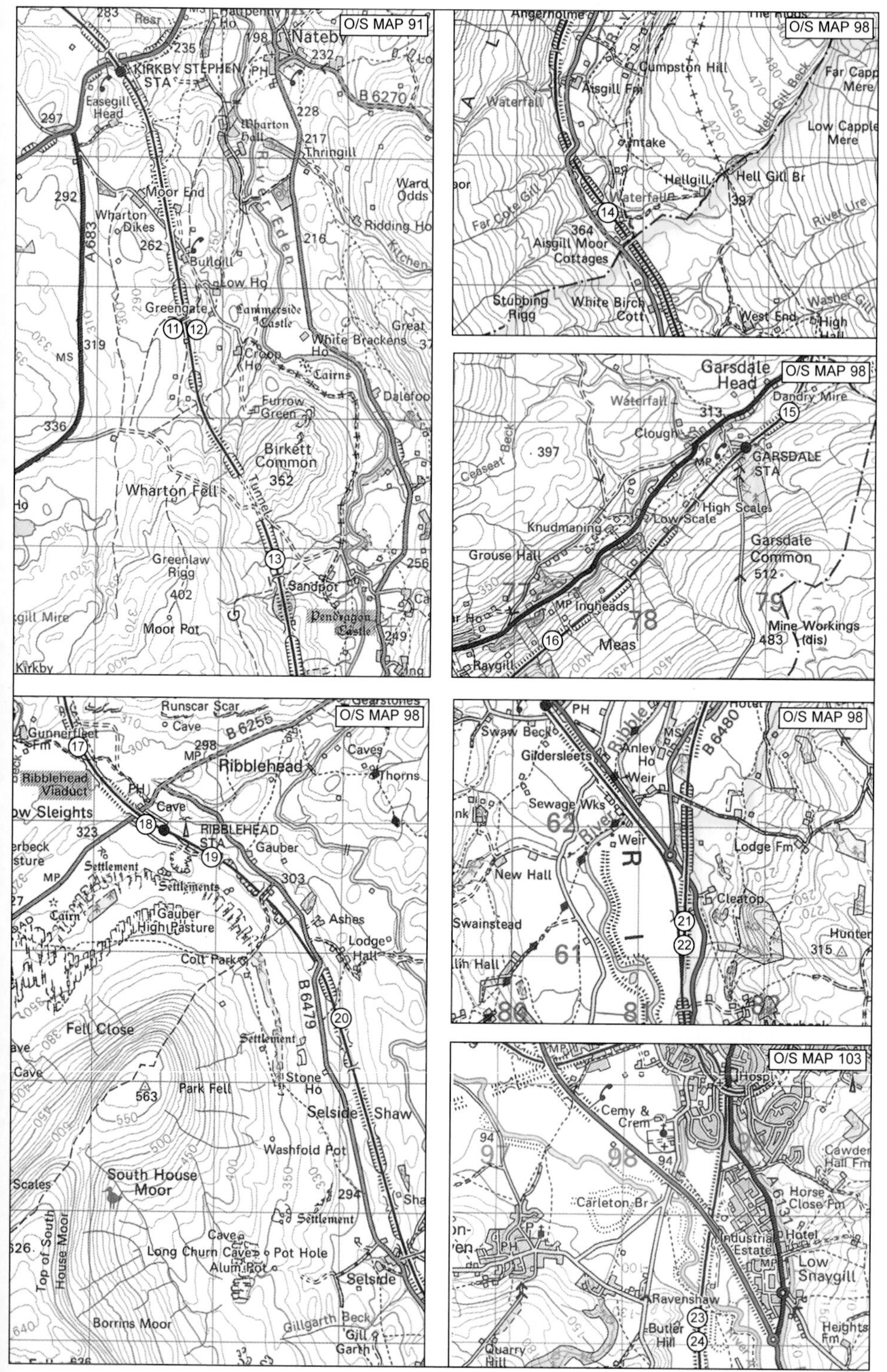

O/S MAP 91
Nateby
KIRKBY STEPHEN STA
B 6270
Easegill Head
Wharton Hall
River Eden
Thringill
Moor End
Wharton Dikes
Ward Odds
Ridding Ho
A 683
Bullgill
Low Ho
Greengate
Lammerside Castle
Croop Ho
White Brackens Ho
Cairns
Furrow Green
Birkett Common
Wharton Fell
Tunnel
Greenlaw Rigg
Sandpot
Moor Pot
Pendragon Castle
O/S MAP 98
Angerholme
Cumpston Hill
Aisgill Fm
Waterfall
Intake
Hellgill
Hell Gill Br
Hell Gill Beck
Far Capple Mere
Low Capple Mere
Far Cote Gill
River Ure
Aisgill Moor Cottages
Stubbing Rigg
White Birch Cott
West End
O/S MAP 98
Garsdale Head
Dandry Mire
Waterfall
Clough
Cegseat Beck
GARSDALE STA
High Scale
Low Scale
Knudmaning
Grouse Hall
Garsdale Common
Ingheads
Meas
Mine Workings (dis)
Raygill
O/S MAP 98
Runscar Scar
Cave
B 6255
Gunnerfleet Fm
Ribblehead
Caves
Thorns
Ribblehead Viaduct
RIBBLEHEAD STA
Gauber
Settlement
Settlements
Cairn
Gauber High Pasture
Ashes
Lodge Hall
Colt Park
B 6479
Fell Close
Settlement
Stone Ho
Park Fell
Selside Shaw
Washfold Pot
South House Moor
Settlement
Top of South House Moor
Cave
Long Churn Cave
Pot Hole
Alum Pot
Selside
Borrins Moor
Gillgarth Beck
Gill Garth
O/S MAP 98
Swaw Beck
Gildersleets
Anley Ho
Weir
B 6480
Sewage Wks
River Ribble
Lodge Fm
New Hall
Cleatop
Swainstead
O/S MAP 103
Hospl
Cemy & Crem
Cawder Hall Fm
A 6131
Carleton Br
Horse Close Fm
Industrial Estate
Hotel
Low Snaygill
Ravenshaw
Butler Hill
Heights Fm
Quarry Hill

(11) **BIRKETT COMMON** : In Spring 2002, Freightliner Heavy Haul broke new ground by running Anglo-Scottish coal trains over the S & C. Passing through Birkett Common, or Wharton as the area is often referred to, one of the first services is seen on an embankment amidst typical fell-like scenery and 66547 (*above*) heading 4Z42, the 0230 Drakelow - Hunterston empties. (RA 03/02)

(12) Looking in the same direction, but this time from the opposite side of the line, we see one of the most popular trains to run over the S & C in recent years; 6M90, the (SO) Gascoigne Wood - Carlisle working of containerised coal for destinations in Scotland. On a delightful Spring evening, 56063 *Bardon Hill* (*below*) is pictured in Birkett Common on 6M90 with a mix of red and green 'tubs' (RA 04/99)

(13) **BIRKETT COMMON** : In the cutting, south of Birkett Tunnel, 156454+156475 make their way into Mallerstang Common, forming the 1426 Arriva Trains service from Carlisle to Leeds. (RA 08/03)

(14) **AIS GILL** : With the unmistakable mass of Wild Boar Fell providing the backdrop, a pair of type 3s (37407 *Blackpool Tower* + 37416) near the end of their climb to Ais Gill summit with the 1110 Glasgow Central - Wolverhampton Regency rail cruise. This train was in connection with the Edinburgh Tattoo and running some 95 minutes late by the time it met up with the photographer! (PJR 08/98)

(15) **GARSDALE** : This is what makes the Settle & Carlisle so special; stunning scenery, architectural wonders and semaphore signals! This view encapsulates the lot as 66015 (*above*), having crossed Dandry Mire viaduct, sweeps round the curve into Garsdale station with 6E13, Newbiggin - Knottingley empty Gypsum containers. (MB 03/03)

(16) During 2002, the daily departmental service from Crewe Basford Hall to Carlisle (6C02) was routed over the S & C, although it could run via the WCML. Heading north, 56099 (*below*) is pictured hauling 6C02 near Garsdale at the site where the water troughs were located in steam days. (RA 09/02)

(17) **RIBBLEHEAD** : During the early 1980s, it was thought the Settle & Carlisle line might close as a result of the poor state of the most impressive structure on the route - Ribblehead (Batty Moss) viaduct. Fortunately, this did not materialise as we can see in this view of 60004 (*above*) crossing the viaduct with 6E13, Newbiggin - Knottingley Gypsum empties. (JW 08/97)

(18) Having left the viaduct, 47769 *Resolve* (*below*) is seen on the embankment, which carries the line over the B6255 road, in charge of 1M28, the diverted 1050 Glasgow - Euston "Royal Scot". The red liveried Virgin Mark 3 coaches really stand out against a partially snow clad Whernside. (JW 01/00)

(19) **RIBBLEHEAD STATION** : The striking black and orange Loadhaul livery is shown off to good effect on 60007, seen passing through Ribblehead station with southbound Gypsum empties. There is also plenty of interest in the picture; not to mention 'the viaduct' and Whernside, but the line which leads to Ribblehead quarry and the new temporary platform constructed on the downside of the line. (PJR 06/96)

(20) **SELSIDE** : The Winter 2003/4 timetable saw the welcome reintroduction of diesel-hauled passenger services on the S & C by Arriva Trains, albeit restricted to a solitary 'out and back' turn worked by top 'n' tail class 37s. At Selside, with dark, threatening, storm clouds gathering over Pen-y-ghent, 37405 brings up the rear of 1E23, the 1333 Carlisle - Leeds service. The train loco. is 37408 *Loch Rannoch*. (RA 10/03)

(21) **SETTLE JUNCTION** : This location affords many vantage points to view S & C passenger/freight trains and two are illustrated here. Having descended the 'Long Drag', Freightliner's 66553 (*above*) passes freshly cut grass in the field below as it slows on the approach to the junction with 6Z49, the 0555 Killoch - Cottam power station service formed of loaded Heavy Haul coal hoppers. (MB 07/03)

(22) During Sunday diversions off the WCML, the first daytime southbound service to leave Carlisle is 1M64, the 1349 Carlisle - Euston, seen here behind 47854 (*below*) at Settle Junction, alongside the 'Little North Western' lines which lead to/from Carnforth. (MB 03/03)

(23) **SNAYGILL** : At Snaygill, just south of Skipton, we see an unidentified member of one of Semen's excellent Class 333 electric units (*above*) passing waterlogged fields in the Aire Valley with a local Skipton - Leeds/ Bradford Forster Square service. (JW 02/01)

(24) A train long associated with the Aire Valley is the distinctive white Tilcon hoppers which convey stone from the Rylestone quarry, north of Skipton. This panoramic view shows 60047 at Snaygill with a rake of 18 empty hoppers forming 6D04, Hull Dairycoates - Rylstone. (JW 05/01)

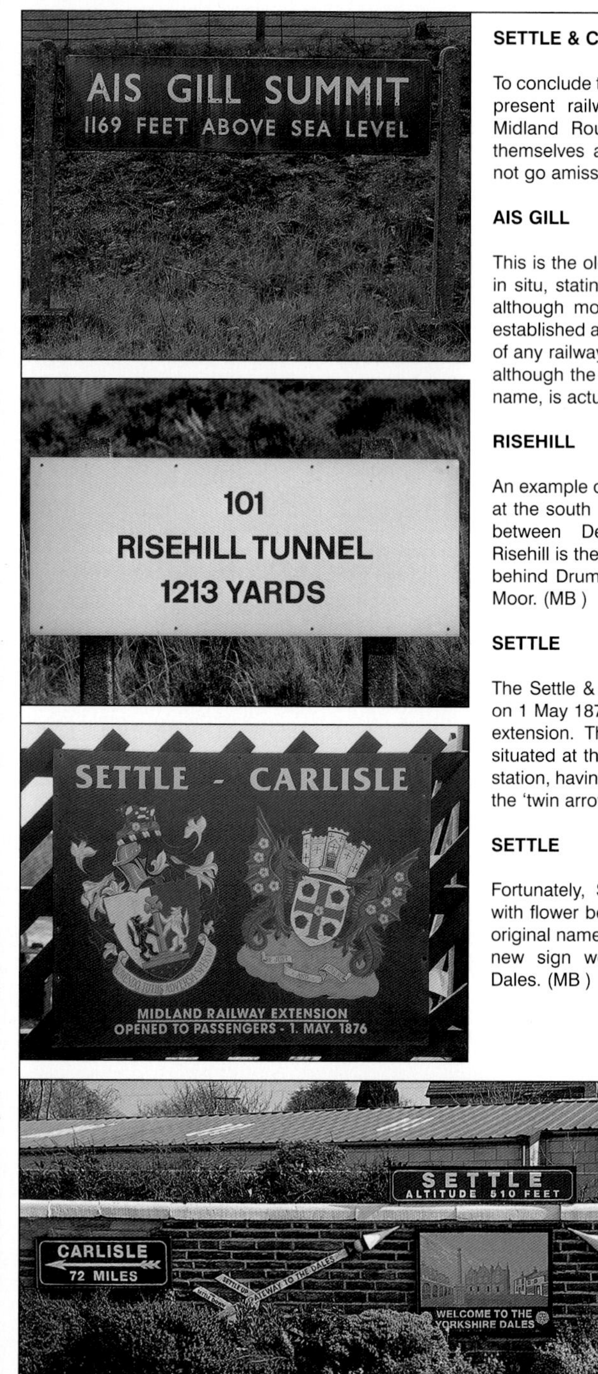

SETTLE & CARLISLE Miscellany ;

To conclude the Gallery section, a selection of past and present railwayana on this famous stretch of the Midland Route. The photographs really speak for themselves although a few accompanying notes will not go amiss. From top to bottom:

AIS GILL

This is the old Midland summit board, sadly no longer in situ, stating an altitude of 1,169ft. above sea level, although more modern measuring instruments have established a height of 1,167ft. This is the highest point of any railway line in England, situated in Ais Gill Moor although the actual 'Gill' from which the moor took its name, is actually about a half mile further north. (MB)

RISEHILL

An example of a modern place board is illustrated here at the south portal of Risehill Tunnel, which is located between Dent and Garsdale. At 1,213 yards long, Risehill is the fifth longest tunnel on the Midland Route behind Drumlanrig, Clay Cross, Wymington and Blea Moor. (MB)

SETTLE

The Settle & Carlisle was opened to passenger traffic on 1 May 1876 and was known as the Midland railway extension. This old Midland nameboard is currently situated at the south end of the 'up' platform at Settle station, having been previously located in the middle of the 'twin arrows' featured below. (MB)

SETTLE

Fortunately, Settle station has remained unchanged with flower beds and the famous twin arrow sign. The original name boards have been replaced along with a new sign welcoming passengers to the Yorkshire Dales. (MB)

Carlisle to Glasgow Central

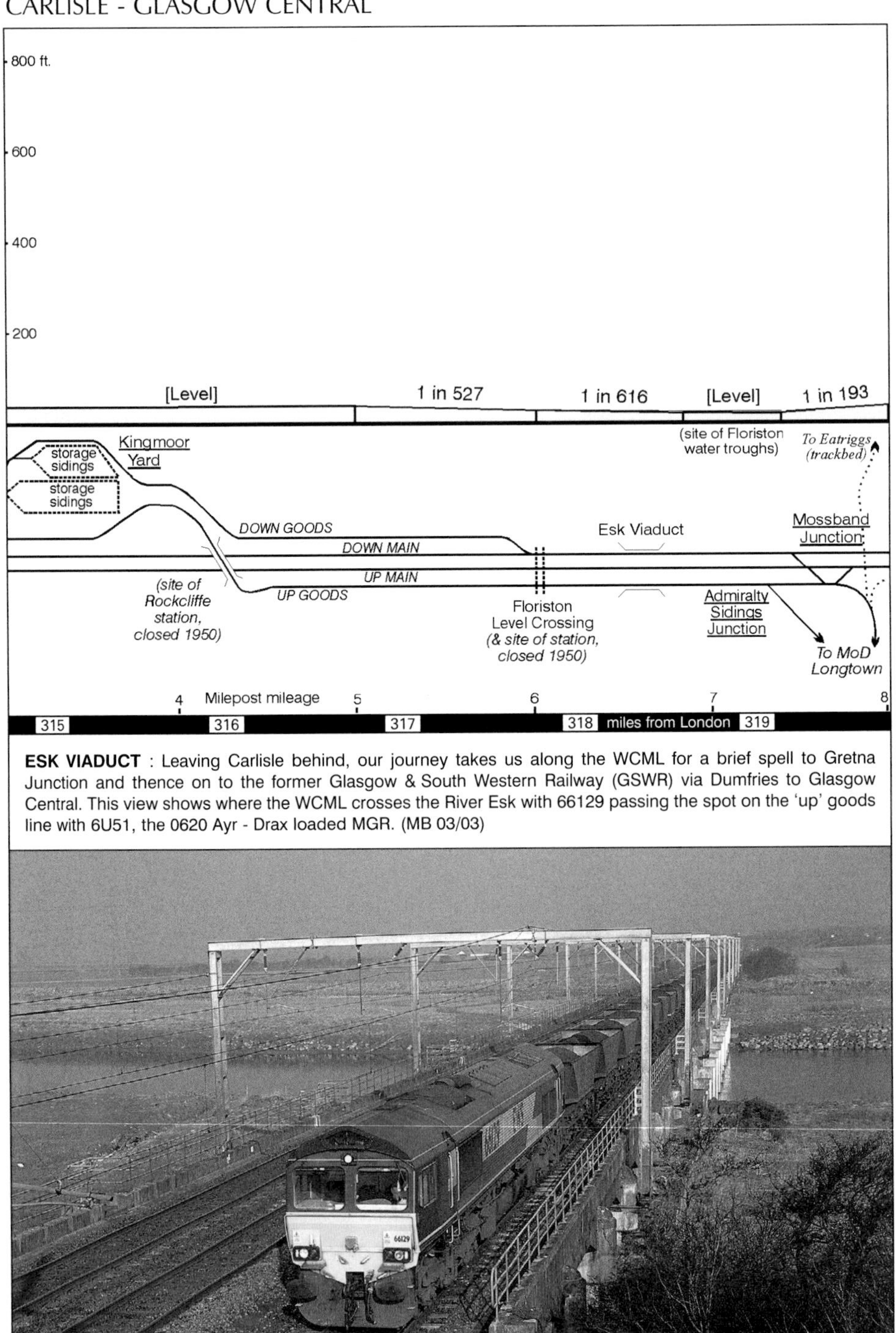

ESK VIADUCT : Leaving Carlisle behind, our journey takes us along the WCML for a brief spell to Gretna Junction and thence on to the former Glasgow & South Western Railway (GSWR) via Dumfries to Glasgow Central. This view shows where the WCML crosses the River Esk with 66129 passing the spot on the 'up' goods line with 6U51, the 0620 Ayr - Drax loaded MGR. (MB 03/03)

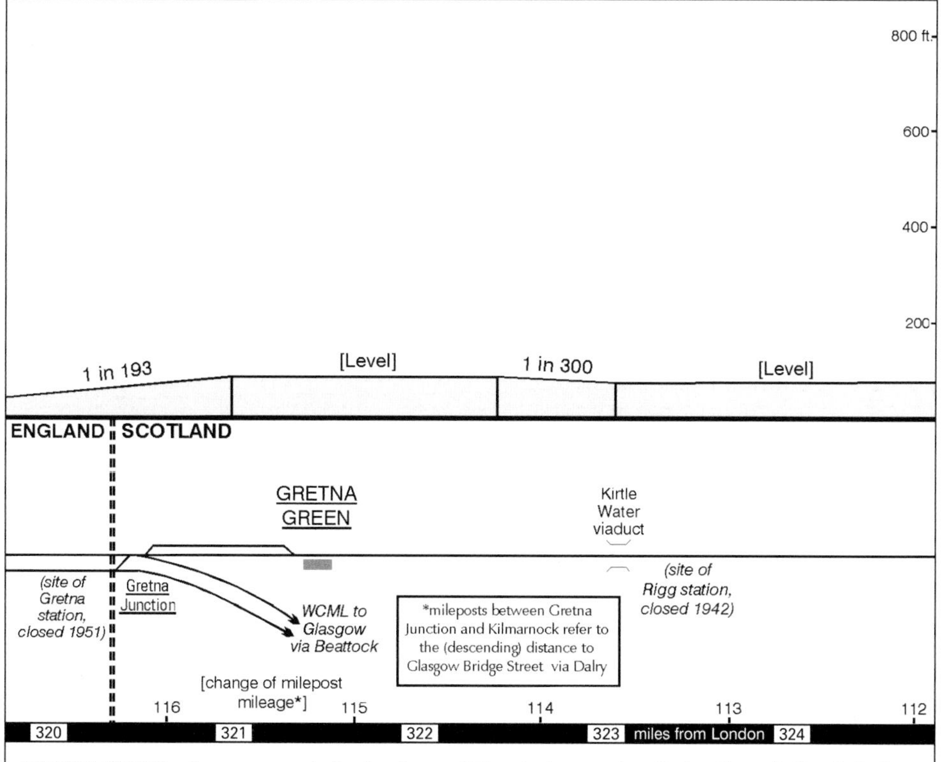

GRETNA GREEN : Famous as a destination for would-be eloping couples, Gretna Green is the start of our journey down the former GSWR, which runs as single track from Gretna Junction to Annan. Coming on to the double track section after making the Gretna Green station stop, 156495 makes its way to the WCML with 1M80, the 0828 Glasgow Central - Carlisle. (MB 03/03)

STONEHOUSE : On the single track section, 37883 is seen at Stonehouse, to the west of Gretna, hauling 6S56, Carlisle Yard - Eastriggs 'Enterprise' trip. (RA 04/99)

EASTRIGGS : A panoramic view shows 66099 leaving the sidings at Eastriggs with a lengthy rake of mostly VGA wagons forming 6M80, Eastriggs - Carlisle 'Enterprise', where the wagons proceed south on the overnight Mossend - Eastleigh 'Enterprise' service. On the horizon, plumes of smoke rise from the cooling towers of Chapelcross power station. (DM 02/00)

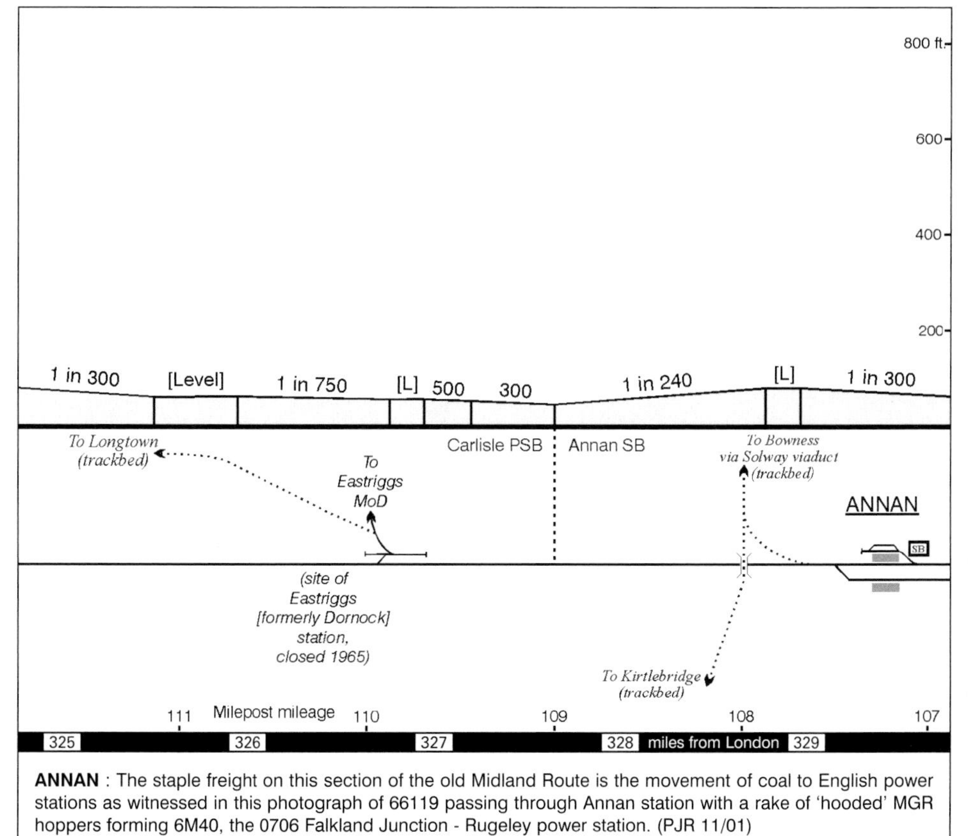

ANNAN : The staple freight on this section of the old Midland Route is the movement of coal to English power stations as witnessed in this photograph of 66119 passing through Annan station with a rake of 'hooded' MGR hoppers forming 6M40, the 0706 Falkland Junction - Rugeley power station. (PJR 11/01)

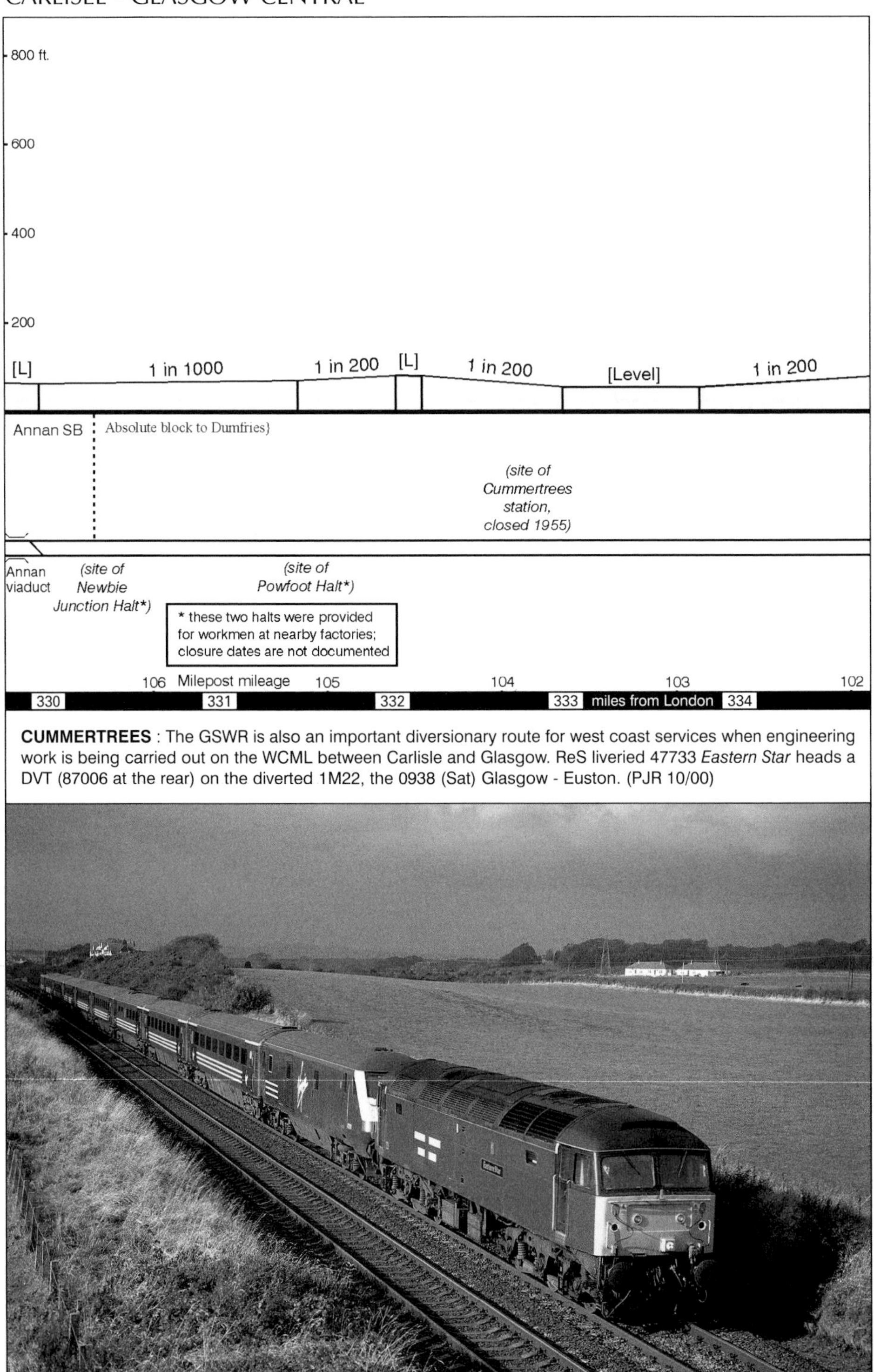

CUMMERTREES : The GSWR is also an important diversionary route for west coast services when engineering work is being carried out on the WCML between Carlisle and Glasgow. ReS liveried 47733 *Eastern Star* heads a DVT (87006 at the rear) on the diverted 1M22, the 0938 (Sat) Glasgow - Euston. (PJR 10/00)

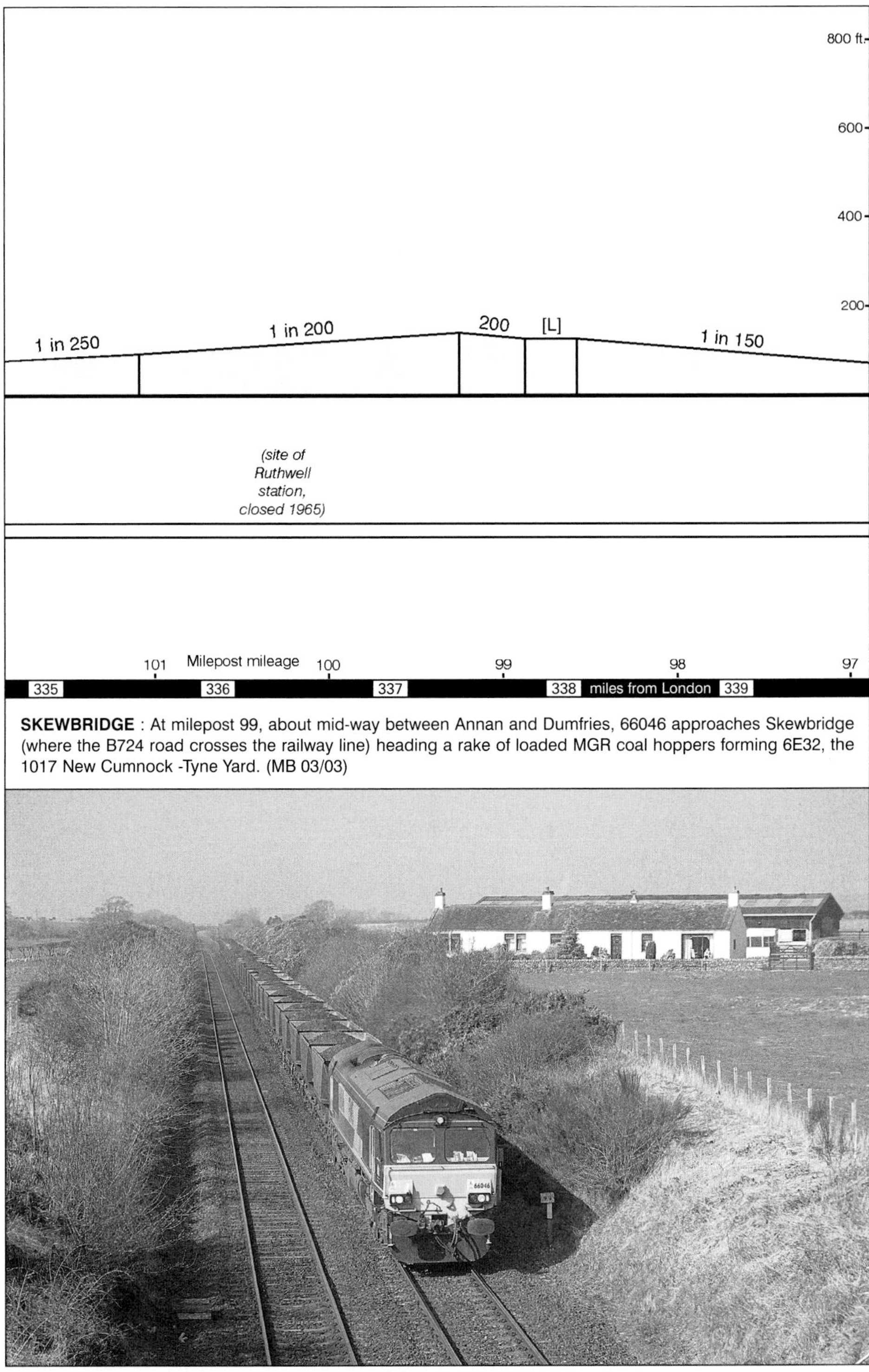

SKEWBRIDGE : At milepost 99, about mid-way between Annan and Dumfries, 66046 approaches Skewbridge (where the B724 road crosses the railway line) heading a rake of loaded MGR coal hoppers forming 6E32, the 1017 New Cumnock -Tyne Yard. (MB 03/03)

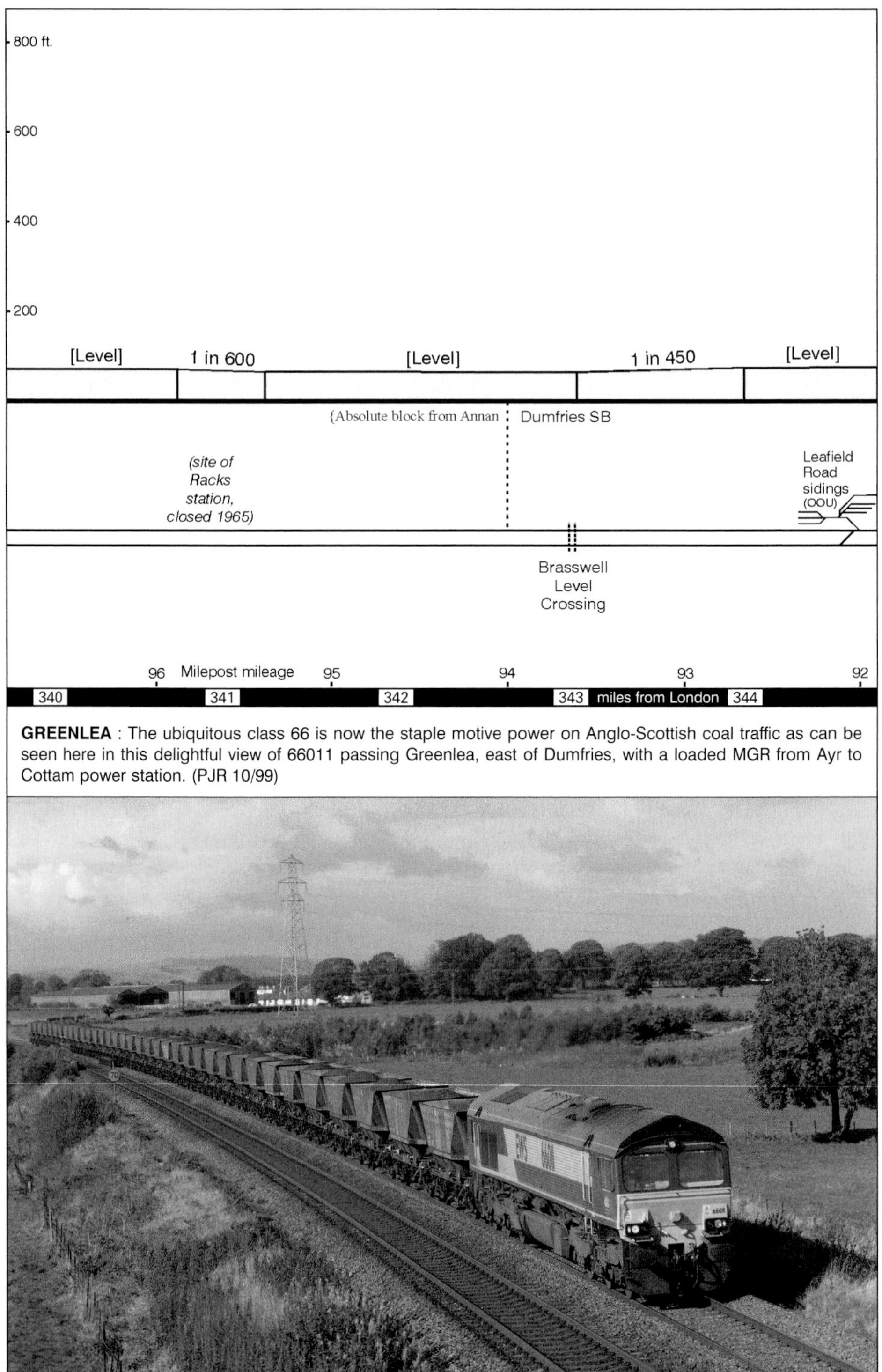

GREENLEA : The ubiquitous class 66 is now the staple motive power on Anglo-Scottish coal traffic as can be seen here in this delightful view of 66011 passing Greenlea, east of Dumfries, with a loaded MGR from Ayr to Cottam power station. (PJR 10/99)

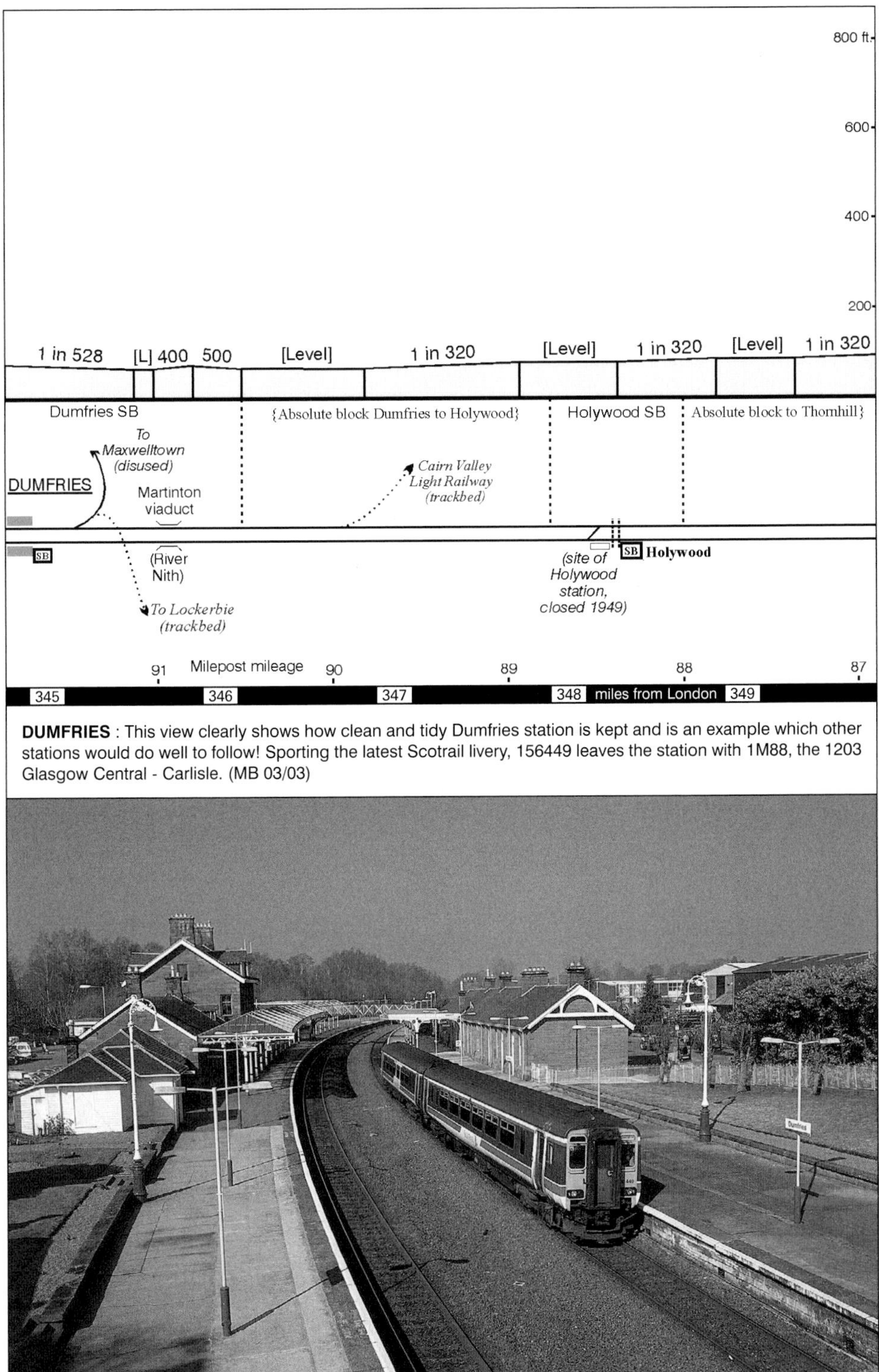

DUMFRIES : This view clearly shows how clean and tidy Dumfries station is kept and is an example which other stations would do well to follow! Sporting the latest Scotrail livery, 156449 leaves the station with 1M88, the 1203 Glasgow Central - Carlisle. (MB 03/03)

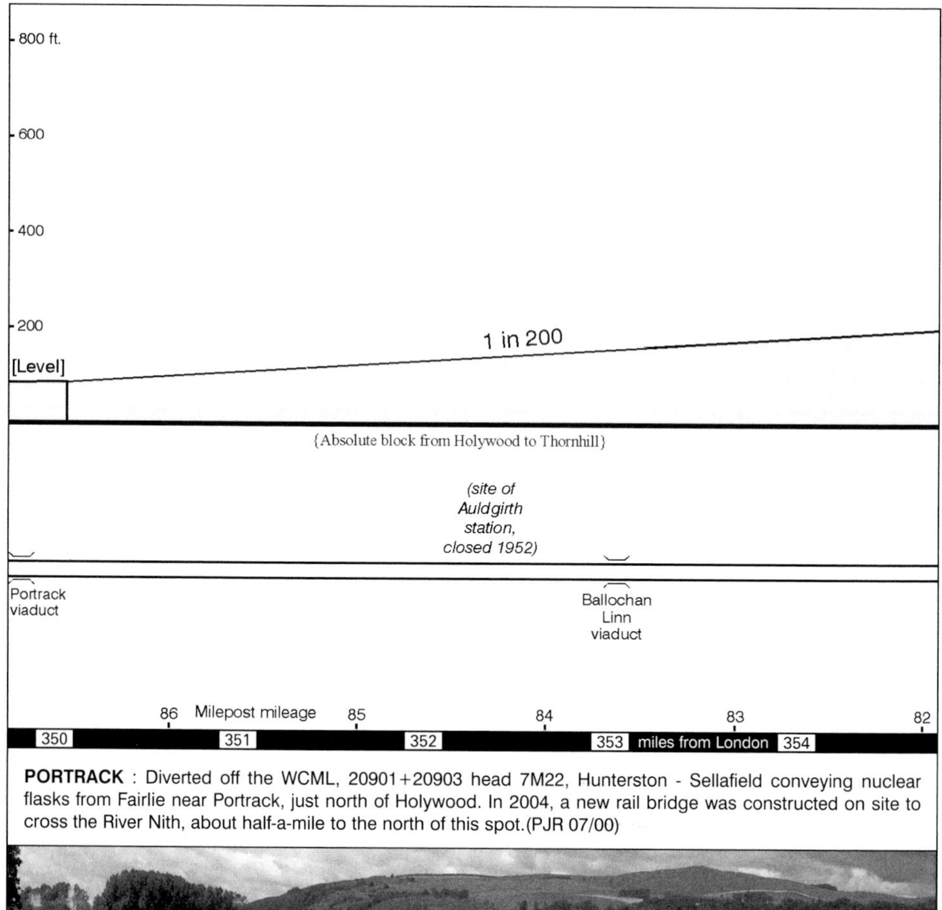

PORTRACK : Diverted off the WCML, 20901+20903 head 7M22, Hunterston - Sellafield conveying nuclear flasks from Fairlie near Portrack, just north of Holywood. In 2004, a new rail bridge was constructed on site to cross the River Nith, about half-a-mile to the north of this spot.(PJR 07/00)

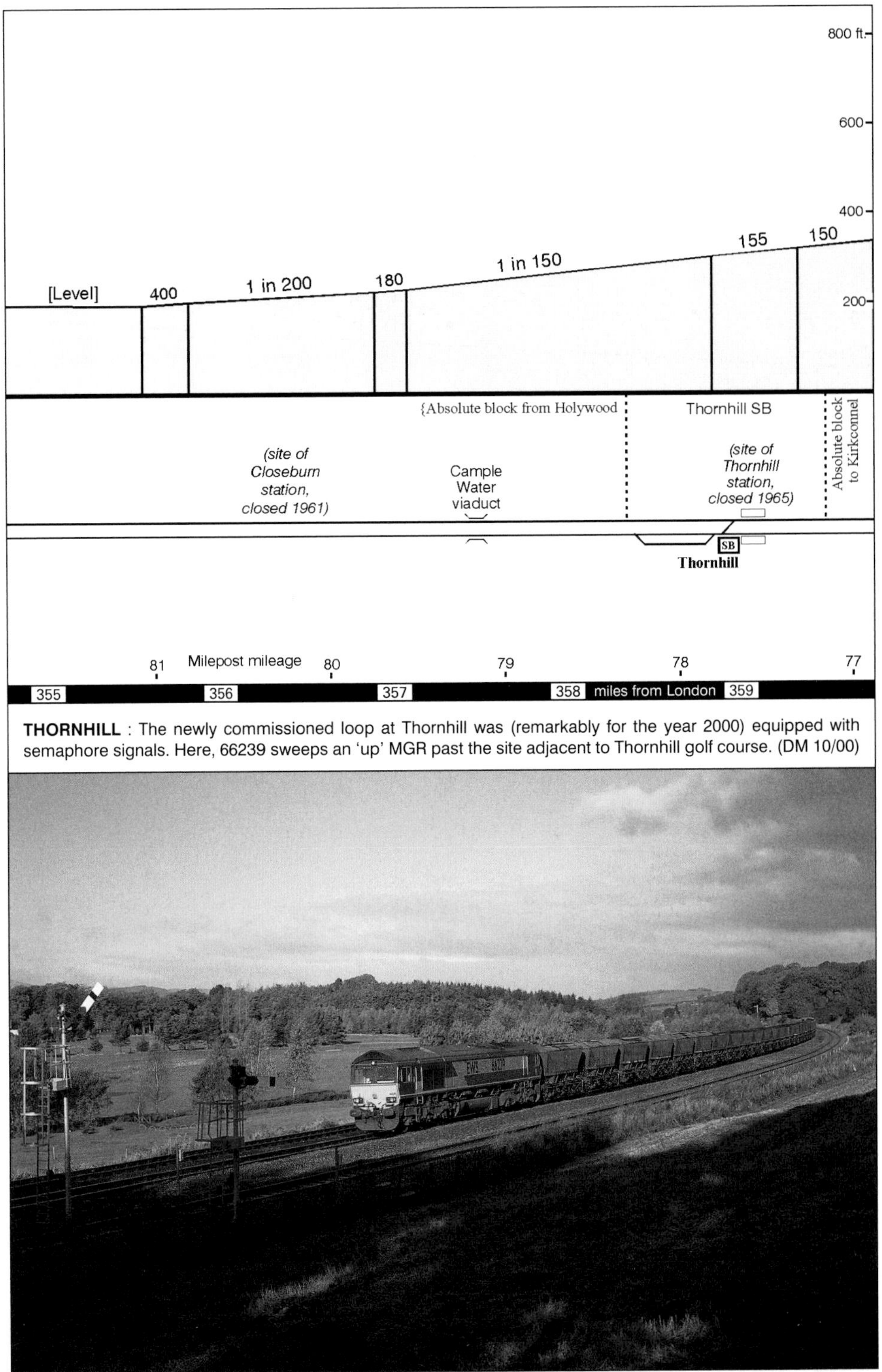

THORNHILL : The newly commissioned loop at Thornhill was (remarkably for the year 2000) equipped with semaphore signals. Here, 66239 sweeps an 'up' MGR past the site adjacent to Thornhill golf course. (DM 10/00)

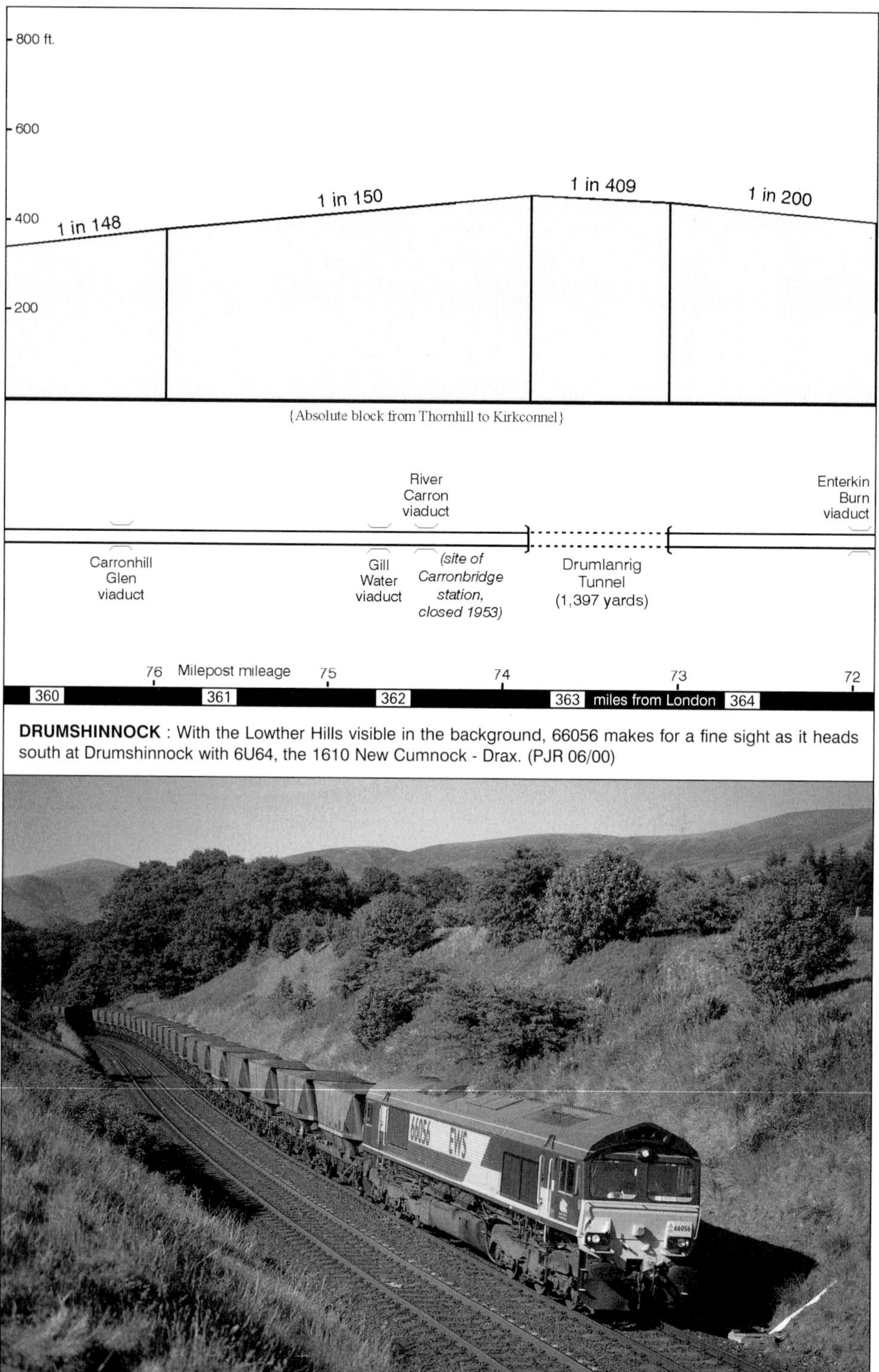

DRUMSHINNOCK : With the Lowther Hills visible in the background, 66056 makes for a fine sight as it heads south at Drumshinnock with 6U64, the 1610 New Cumnock - Drax. (PJR 06/00)

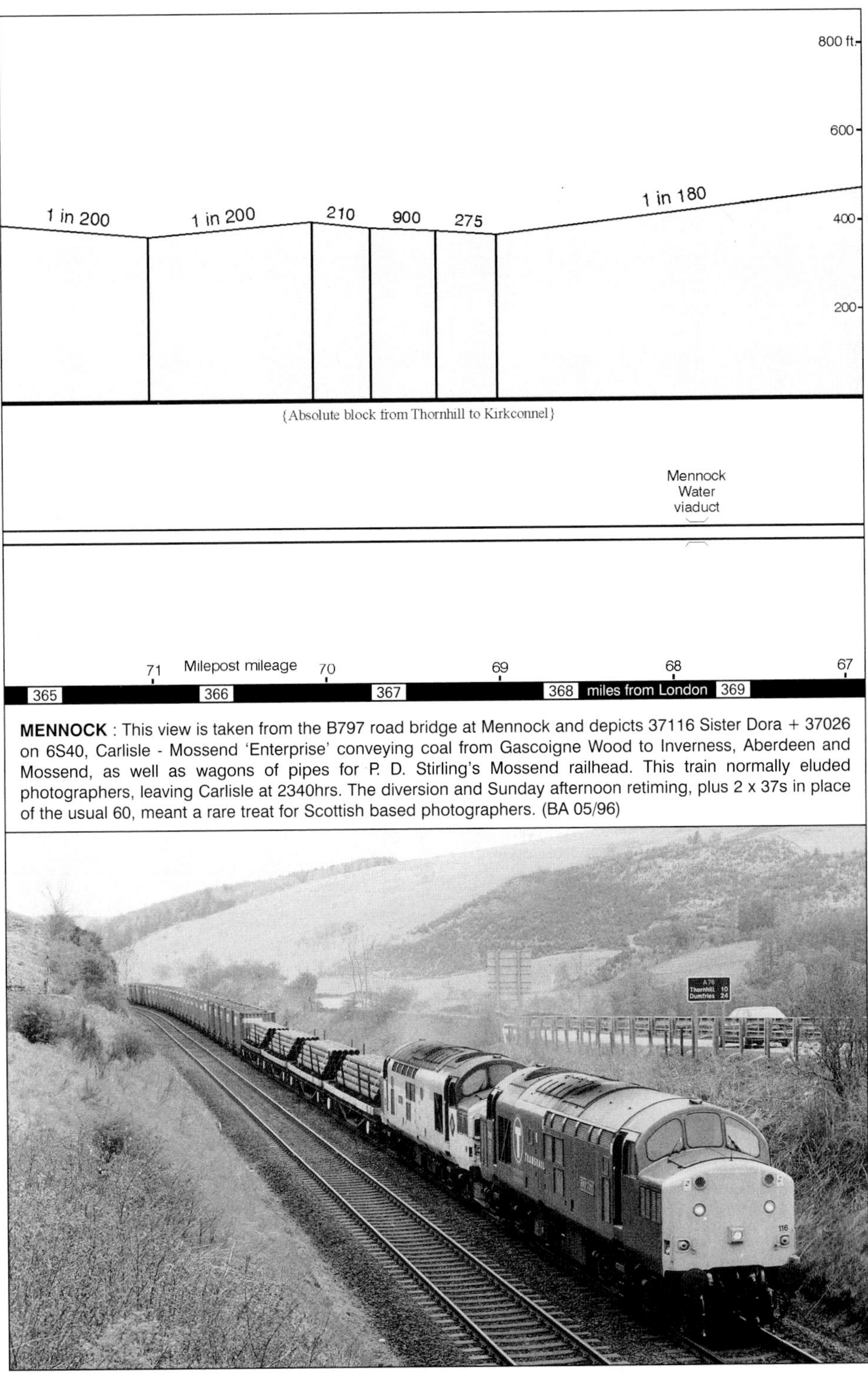

MENNOCK : This view is taken from the B797 road bridge at Mennock and depicts 37116 Sister Dora + 37026 on 6S40, Carlisle - Mossend 'Enterprise' conveying coal from Gascoigne Wood to Inverness, Aberdeen and Mossend, as well as wagons of pipes for P. D. Stirling's Mossend railhead. This train normally eluded photographers, leaving Carlisle at 2340hrs. The diversion and Sunday afternoon retiming, plus 2 x 37s in place of the usual 60, meant a rare treat for Scottish based photographers. (BA 05/96)

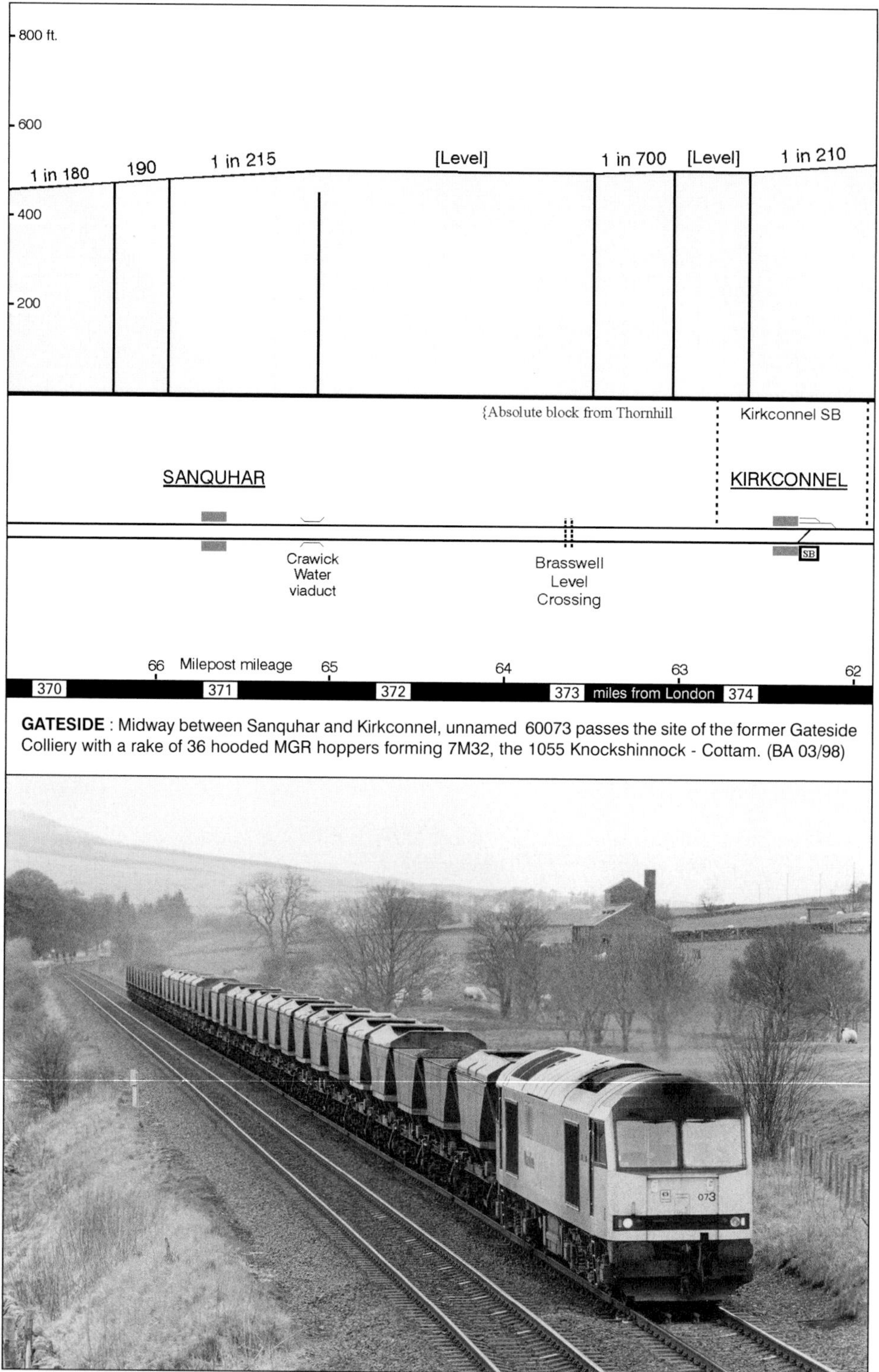

GATESIDE : Midway between Sanquhar and Kirkconnel, unnamed 60073 passes the site of the former Gateside Colliery with a rake of 36 hooded MGR hoppers forming 7M32, the 1055 Knockshinnock - Cottam. (BA 03/98)

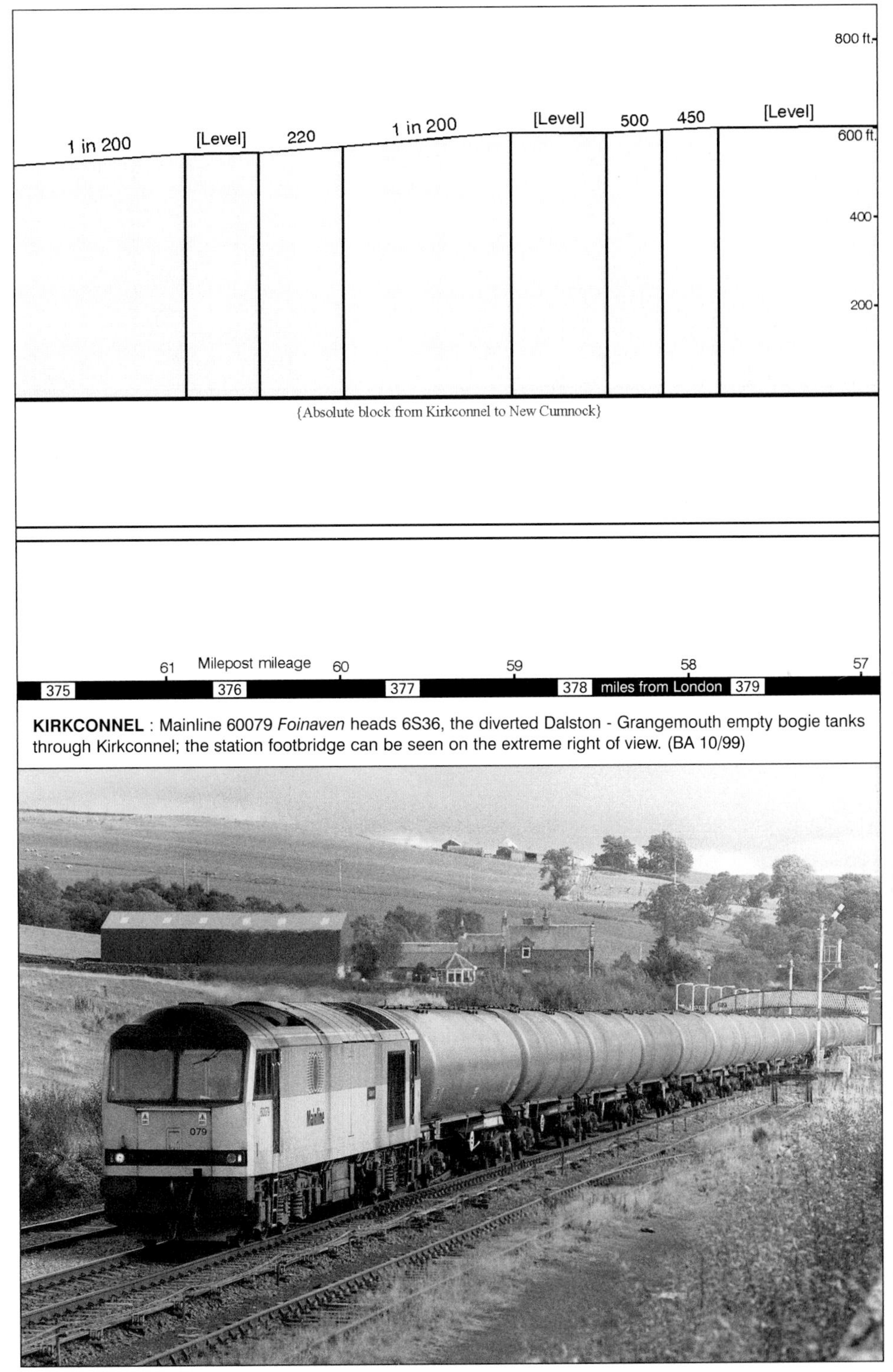

KIRKCONNEL : Mainline 60079 *Foinaven* heads 6S36, the diverted Dalston - Grangemouth empty bogie tanks through Kirkconnel; the station footbridge can be seen on the extreme right of view. (BA 10/99)

NEW CUMNOCK : A contrast of old and new technology .... semaphore signalling and new locomotives! 66237 (*above*) passes through New Cumnock station with a loaded MGR while 66523 is stabled in the recently opened coal loading terminal. It is difficult to get a 'close up' view of the terminal, but this photograph at least shows its existence along with the connection to the up goods loop behind the southbound platform. (RR 03/03)

With the village of New Cumnock in the background, 60031 (*below*) comes off the branch from Knockshinnock Disposal Point onto the northbound G & SW main line at Bank Junction, heading 7M32, the 1055 service to Cottam power station. The train will head north to Falkland Junction (Ayr) to run round, then reversing, heading south again past the same spot in a couple of hours time! (BA 03/98)

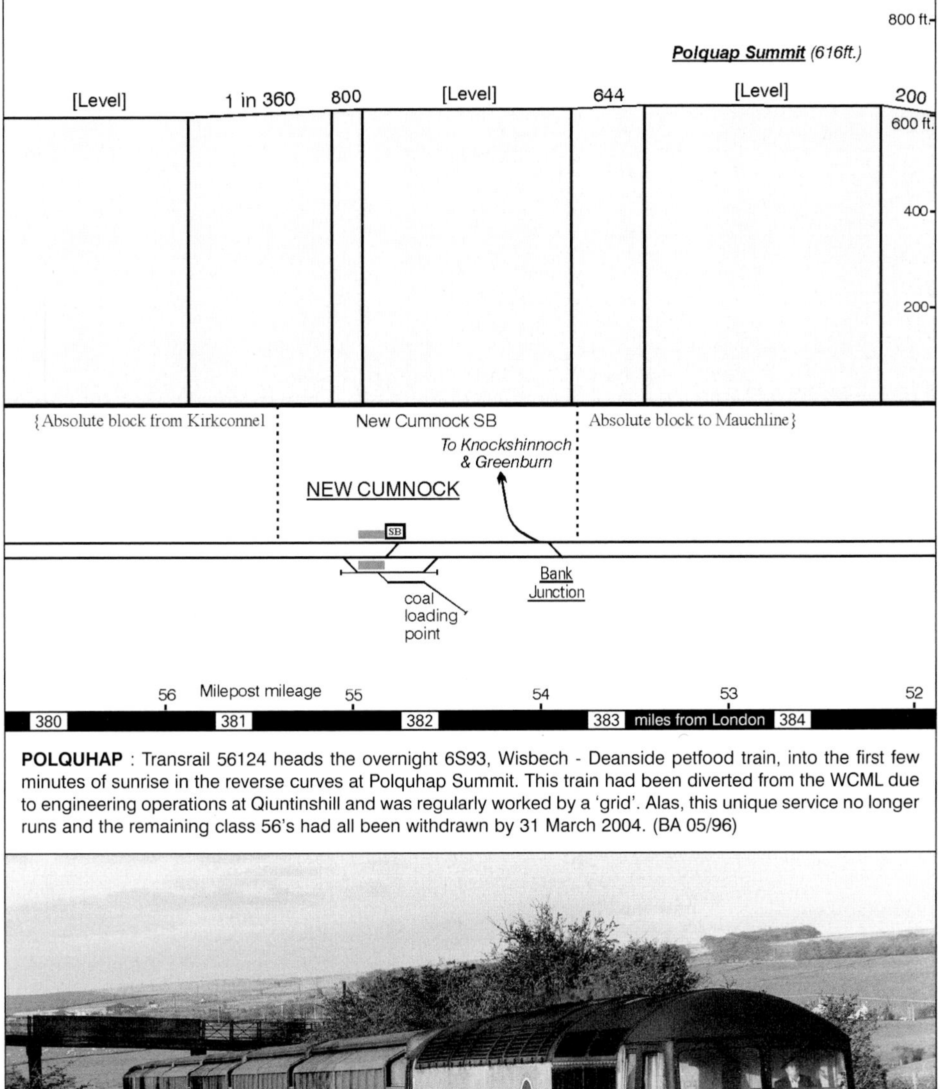

POLQUHAP : Transrail 56124 heads the overnight 6S93, Wisbech - Deanside petfood train, into the first few minutes of sunrise in the reverse curves at Polquhap Summit. This train had been diverted from the WCML due to engineering operations at Qiuntinshill and was regularly worked by a 'grid'. Alas, this unique service no longer runs and the remaining class 56's had all been withdrawn by 31 March 2004. (BA 05/96)

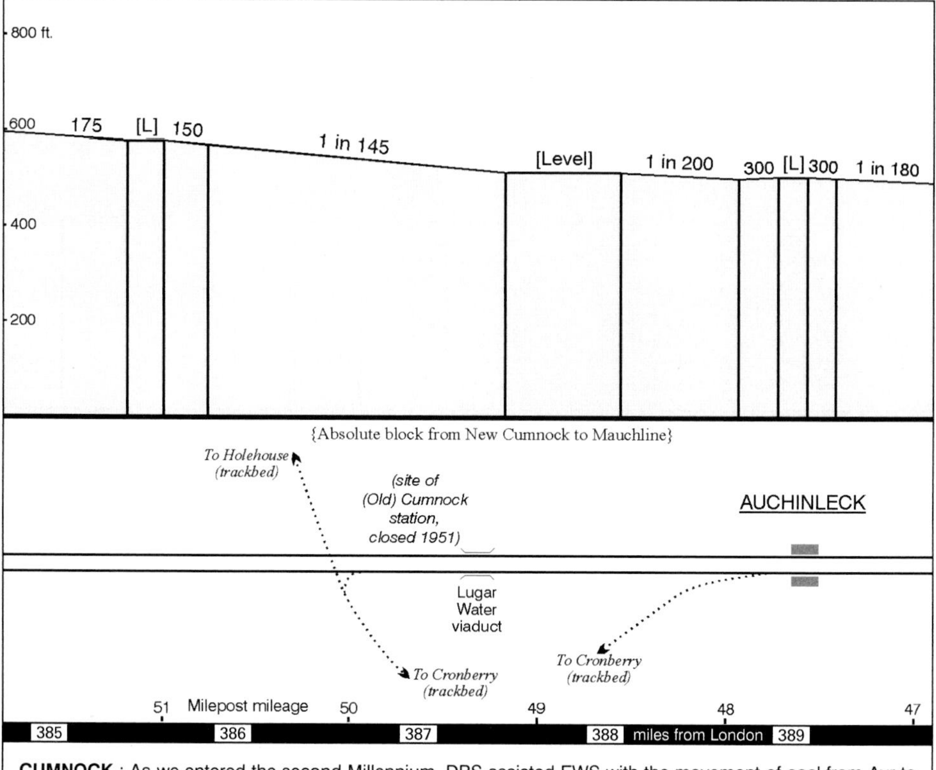

CUMNOCK : As we entered the second Millennium, DRS assisted EWS with the movement of coal from Ayr to Carlisle. One such service is seen here at Craigens, on the outskirts of Cumnock, where 37607+37608 power 6M40, the 0706 Ayr - Carlisle loaded MGR; an EWS class 92 would then take over at Carlisle for the journey south with an EWS 66 taking charge of the final leg from Bescot to one of the West Midlands power stations. (RA 05/00)

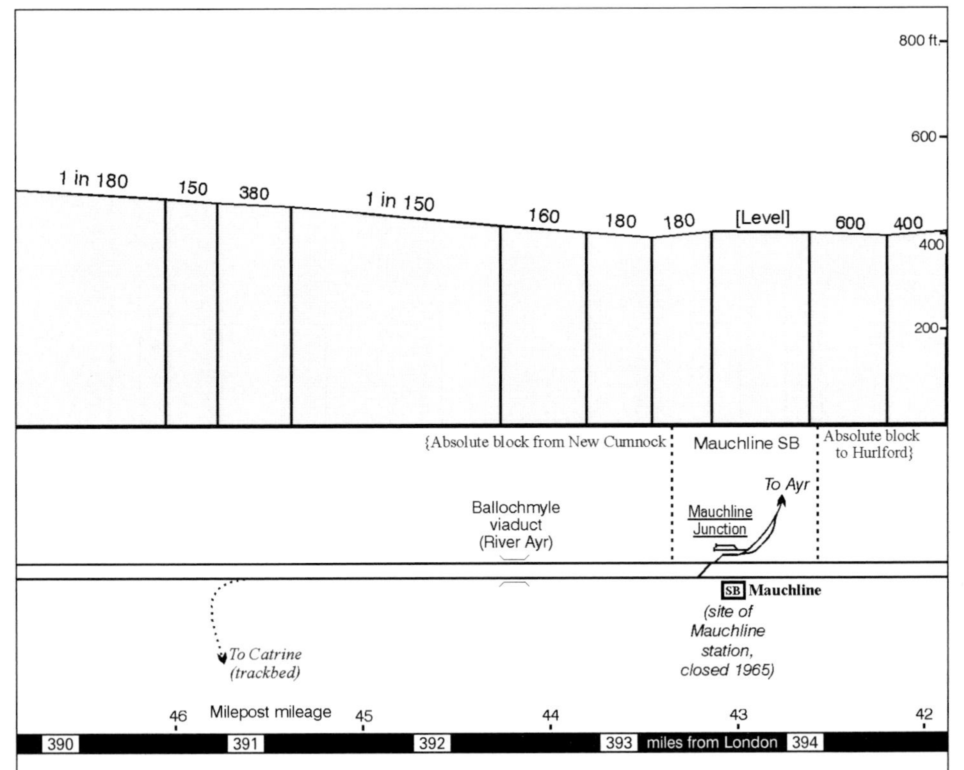

AUCHINLECK : Auchinleck is a rather strange sounding name, meaning 'A field of Flagstones', and home of the great 18th. century biographer James Boswell. At a deserted Auchinleck station, 156457 is seen arriving with the 1000 Stranraer - Newcastle service. (RR 09/02)

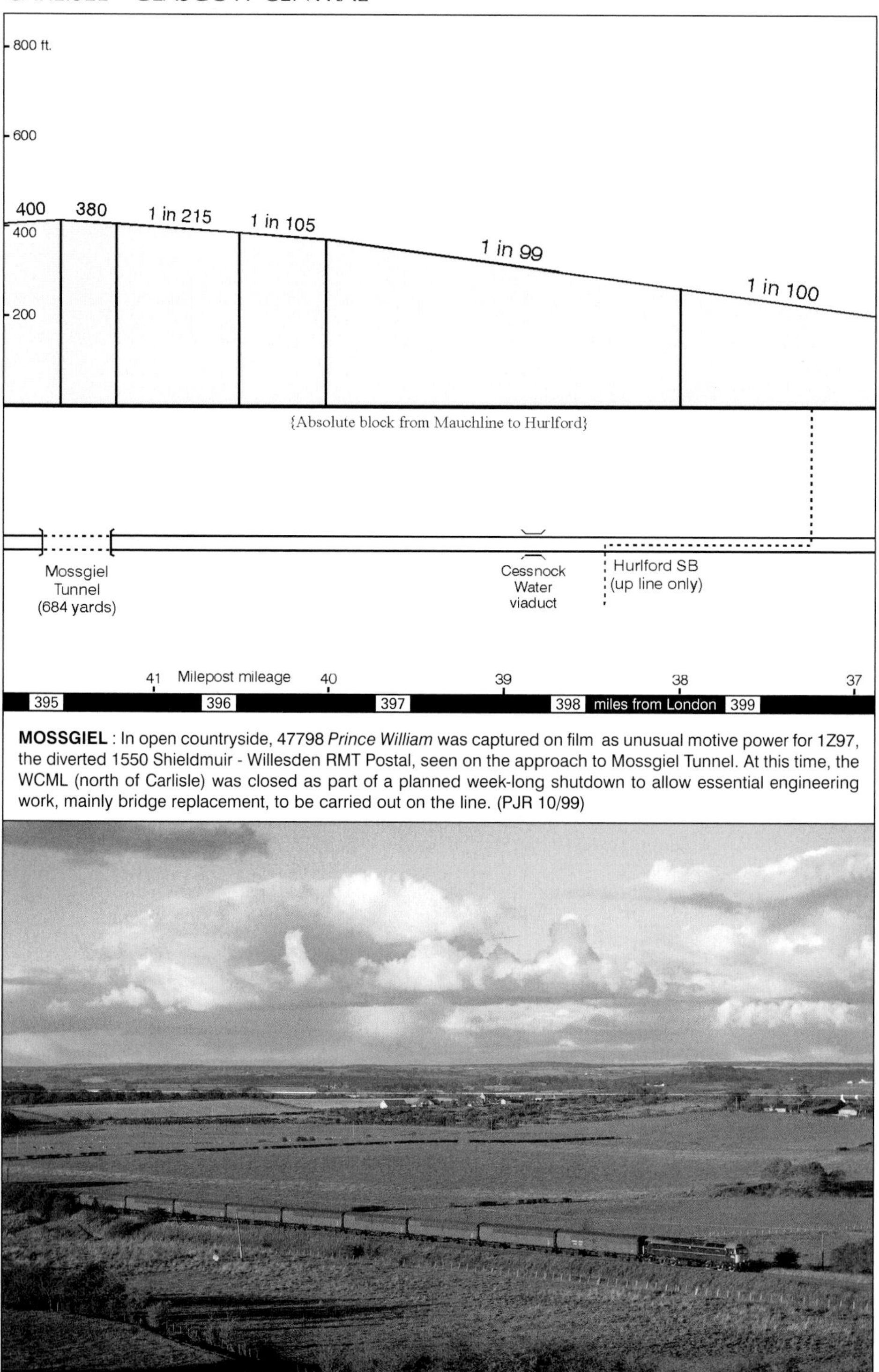

MOSSGIEL : In open countryside, 47798 *Prince William* was captured on film as unusual motive power for 1Z97, the diverted 1550 Shieldmuir - Willesden RMT Postal, seen on the approach to Mossgiel Tunnel. At this time, the WCML (north of Carlisle) was closed as part of a planned week-long shutdown to allow essential engineering work, mainly bridge replacement, to be carried out on the line. (PJR 10/99)

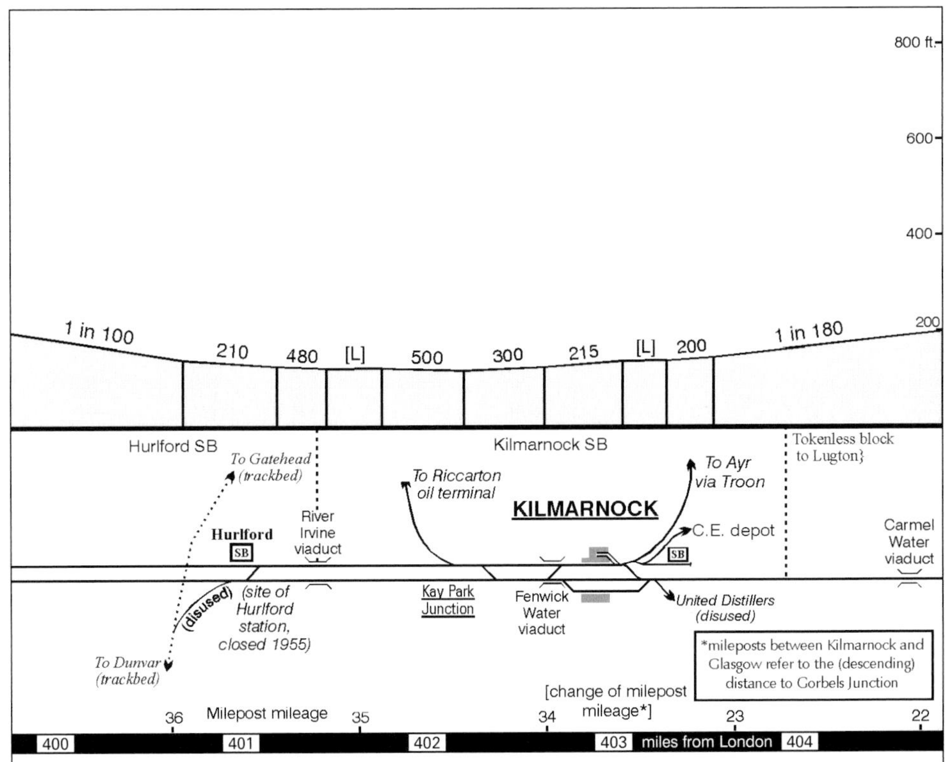

KILMARNOCK : The station at Kilmarnock still retains the original canopy which now spans the two bay platforms along with the 'down' main platform. This is visible in this view of 156432 (*left*) on the 1548 Glasgow Central - Newcastle while 156433 (*right*) awaits departure with the 1631 service to Girvan. From Kilmarnock, the Midland Route continues as single line track before doubling up again at Barrhead. (RR 09/02)

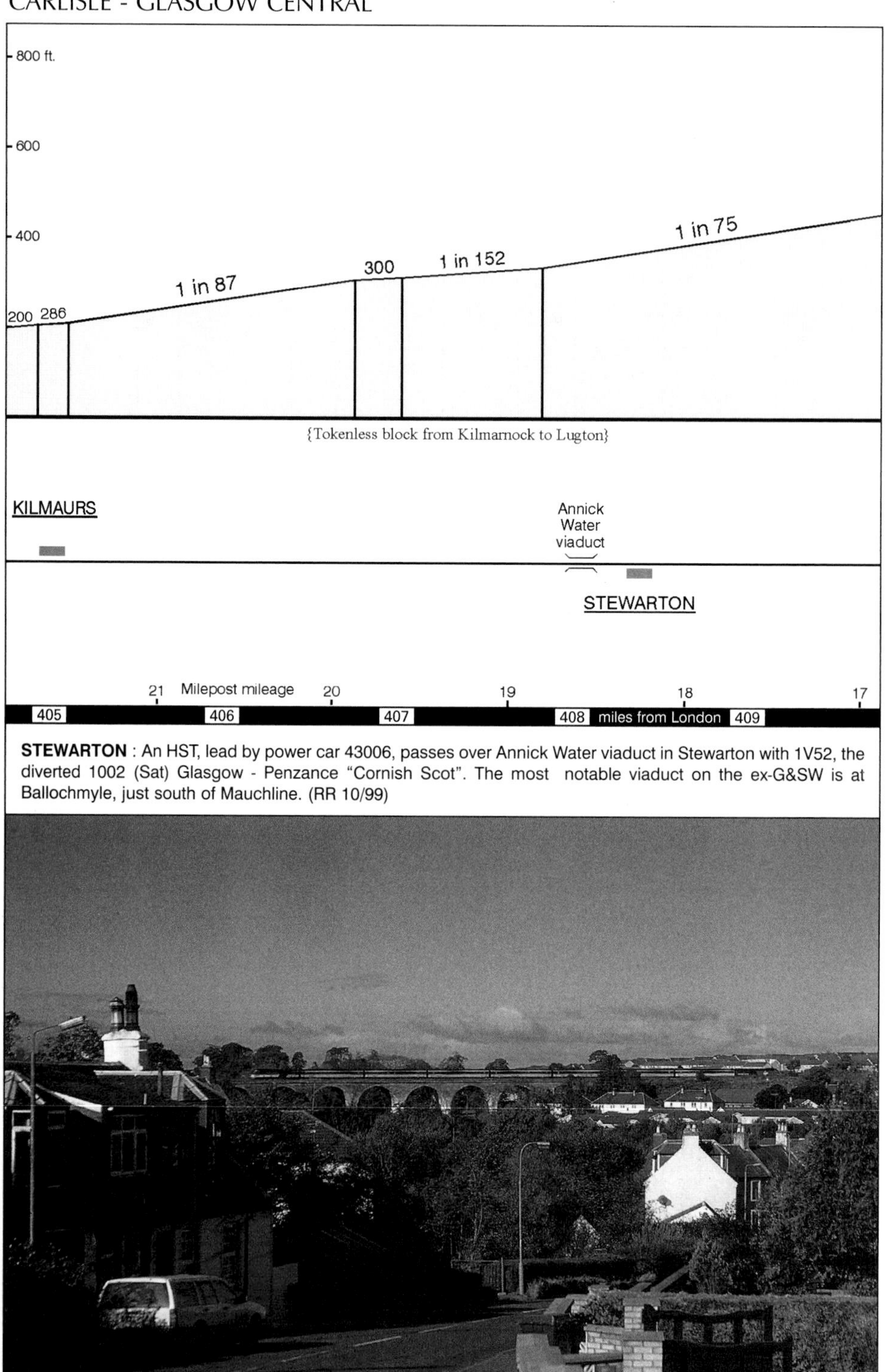

STEWARTON : An HST, lead by power car 43006, passes over Annick Water viaduct in Stewarton with 1V52, the diverted 1002 (Sat) Glasgow - Penzance "Cornish Scot". The most notable viaduct on the ex-G&SW is at Ballochmyle, just south of Mauchline. (RR 10/99)

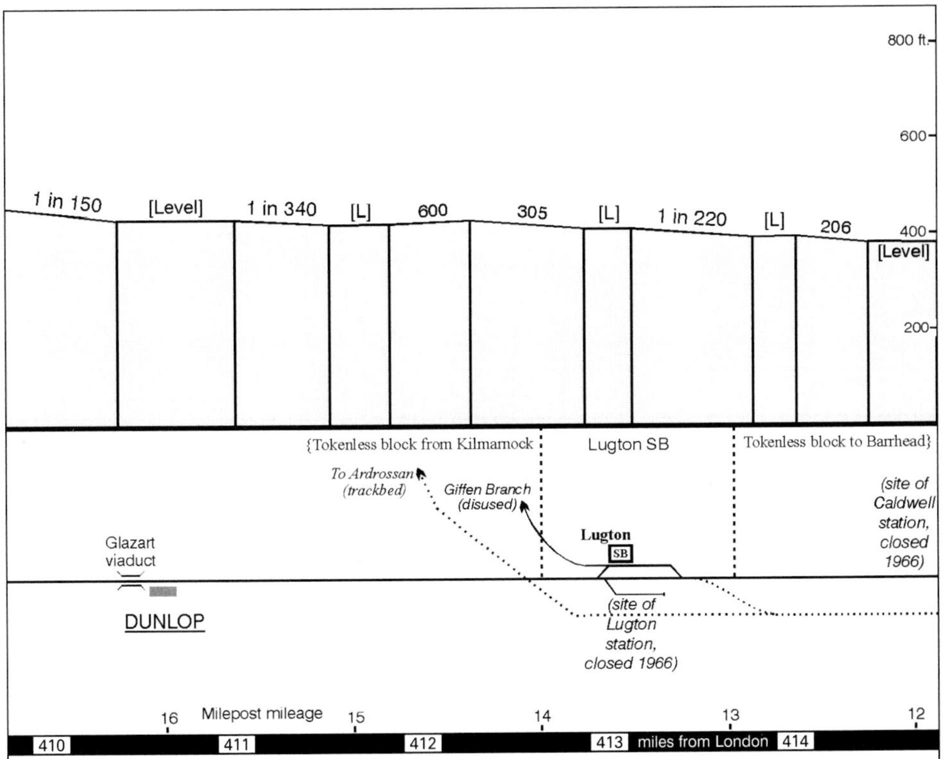

LUGTON : There is single line track between Kilmarnock and Barrhead and 47791 is seen on this section at Lugton with 1M38, the diverted 1730 (Sat) Glasgow - Euston. The train has just passed the trackbed of the former Lanarkshire & Ayrshire Railway, which ran from Neilston to Ardrossan. (RR 08/99)

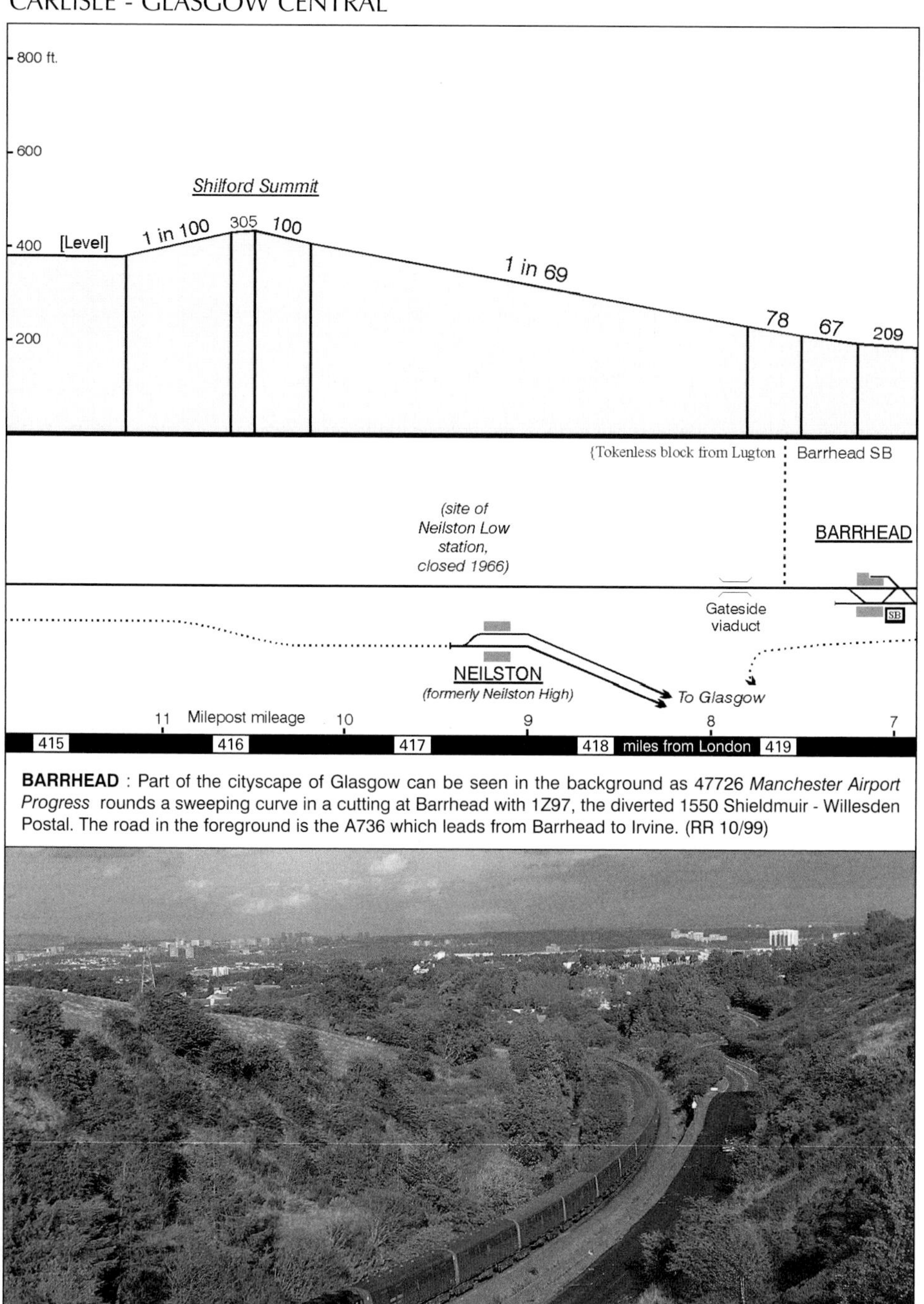

BARRHEAD : Part of the cityscape of Glasgow can be seen in the background as 47726 *Manchester Airport Progress* rounds a sweeping curve in a cutting at Barrhead with 1Z97, the diverted 1550 Shieldmuir - Willesden Postal. The road in the foreground is the A736 which leads from Barrhead to Irvine. (RR 10/99)

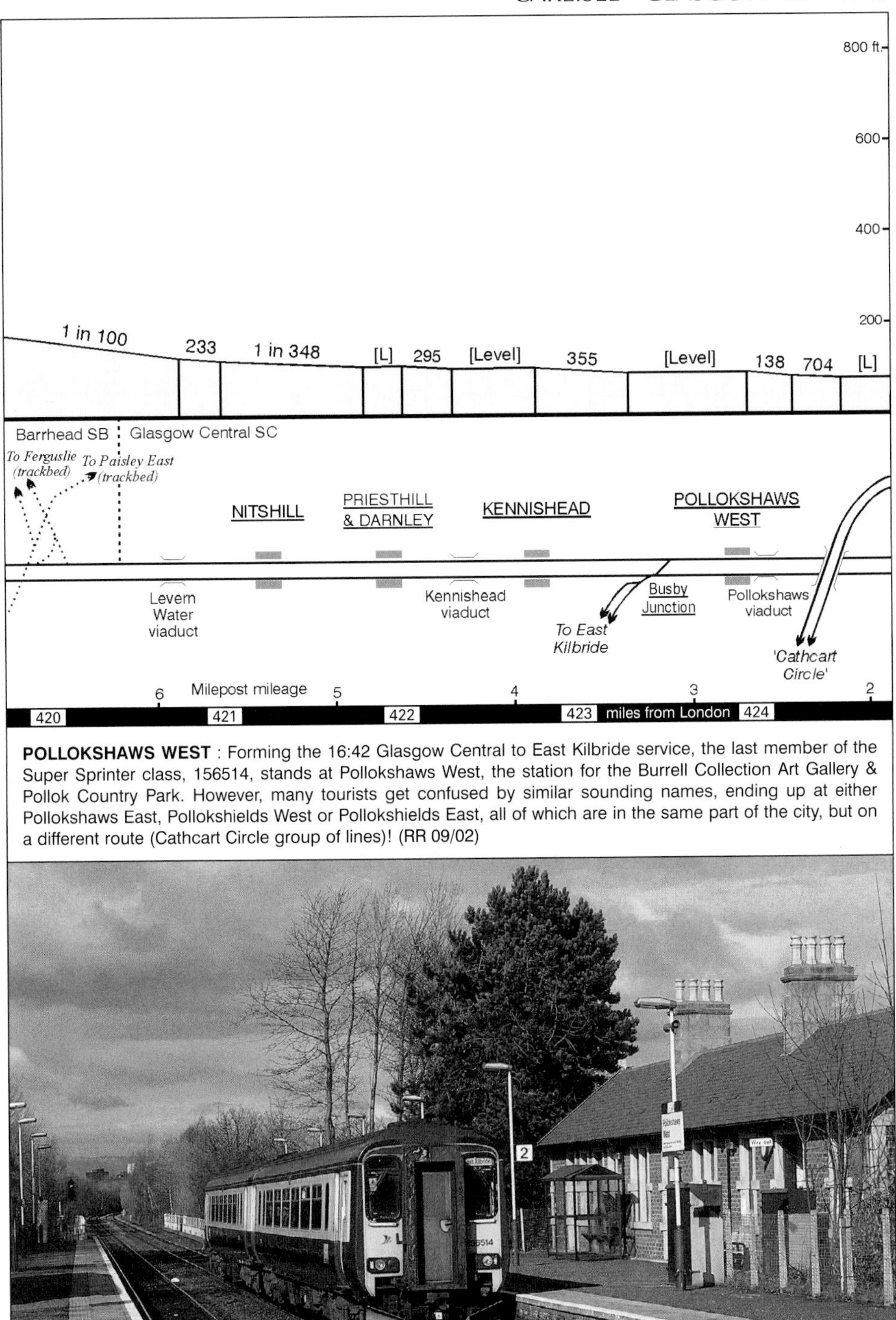

POLLOKSHAWS WEST : Forming the 16:42 Glasgow Central to East Kilbride service, the last member of the Super Sprinter class, 156514, stands at Pollokshaws West, the station for the Burrell Collection Art Gallery & Pollok Country Park. However, many tourists get confused by similar sounding names, ending up at either Pollokshaws East, Pollokshields West or Pollokshields East, all of which are in the same part of the city, but on a different route (Cathcart Circle group of lines)! (RR 09/02)

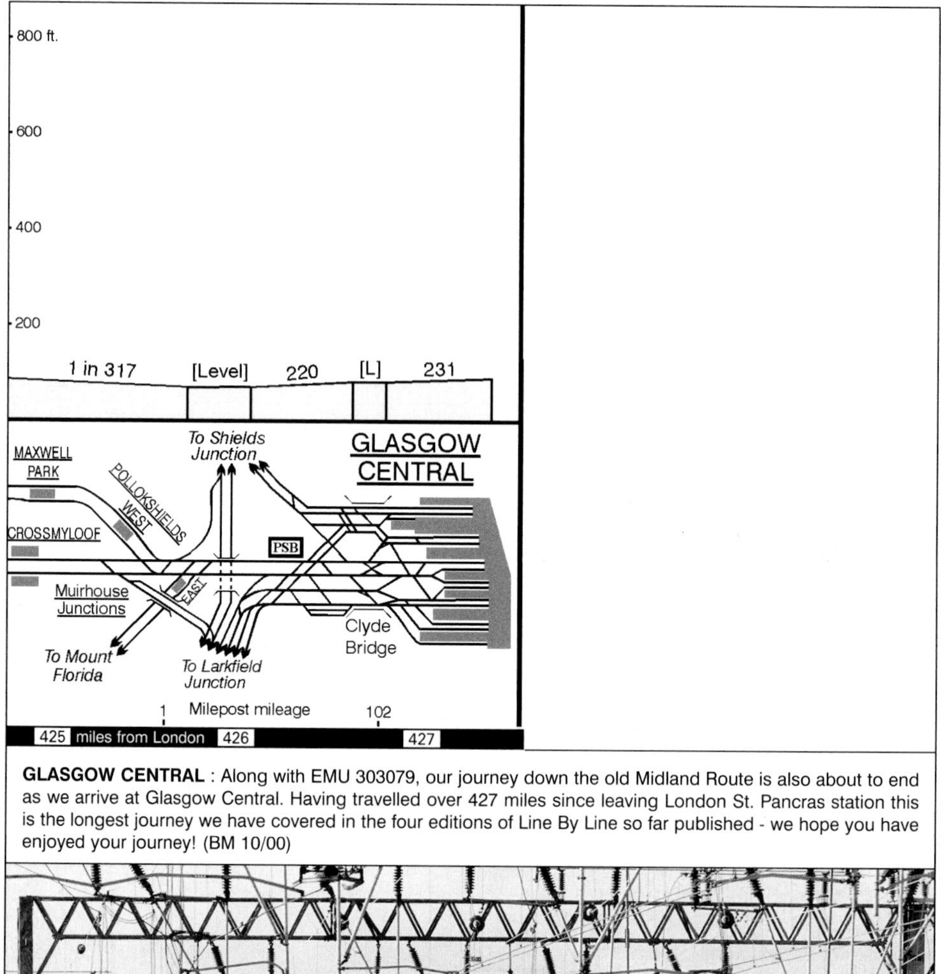

GLASGOW CENTRAL : Along with EMU 303079, our journey down the old Midland Route is also about to end as we arrive at Glasgow Central. Having travelled over 427 miles since leaving London St. Pancras station this is the longest journey we have covered in the four editions of Line By Line so far published - we hope you have enjoyed your journey! (BM 10/00)

Glossary

Miles and Chains

These tables set out the mileage for the Midland Route in the down direction from London St. Pancras to Glasgow Central.

Cumulative Mileage is given in Miles and Chains plus the Local Mileage when local mileposts replace the cumulative ones besides the running lines. Every station, junction and tunnel is listed under Location; stations are highlighted in bold typeface along with a note of the Page Number for reference.

LONDON St. PANCRAS - GLASGOW CENTRAL

Cumulative Mileage	Local Mileage	Location	Page Number
(M. Chs.)	**(M. Chs.)**		
		1. The Midland Mainline	
0.00		**LONDON ST. PANCRAS**	**12**
0.79		*Camden Road Tunnels (south portals)*	
1.13		*Camden Road Tunnels (north portals)*	
1.42		**Kentish Town**	**12**
1.65		*Kentish Town Junction*	
1.74		*Hampstead Tunnel (south portal)*	
1.76		*Hampstead Tunnel (north portal)*	
2.17		*Lismore Circus Tunnel (south portal)*	
2.22		*Lismore Circus Tunnel (north portal)*	
2.29		*Belsize Tunnel up slow line (south portal)*	
2.33		*Belsize Tunnel up fast line (south portal)*	
3.34		*Belsize Tunnels (north portals)*	
3.73		**West Hampstead**	**12**
5.09		**Cricklewood**	**14**
5.19		*Cricklewood Curve Junction*	
6.04		*Brent Curve Junction*	
6.79		**Hendon**	**14**
7.72		*Silkstream Junction*	
9.28		**Mill Hill Broadway**	**14**
11.38		*Elstree Tunnels (south portals)*	
12.06		*Elstree Tunnels (north portals)*	
12.35		**Elstree & Borehamwood**	**15**
15.17		**Radlett**	**16**
19.71		**St. Albans City**	**17**
24.51		**Harpenden**	**17**
29.19		**Luton Airport Parkway**	**18**
30.19		**Luton**	**19**
32.60		**Leagrave**	**19**
37.22		**Harlington**	**20**
40.18		**Flitwick**	**21**
42.19		*Ampthill Tunnels (south portals)*	
42.52		*Ampthill Tunnels (north portals)*	

(M.Ch)	(M. Ch)	Location	Page
49.65		**BEDFORD MIDLAND**	**23**
56.45		**Sharnbrook Summit**	
59.00		*Sharnbrook (Wymington) Tunnel (south portal)*	
60.04		*Sharnbrook (Wymington Tunnel (north portal)*	
65.11		**WELLINGBOROUGH**	**26**
72.01		**KETTERING**	**27**
74.00		*Kettering North Junction*	
82.74		**MARKET HARBOROUGH**	**29**
88.71		***Kibworth Summit***	
95.37		*Wigston South Junction*	
95.76		*Wigston North Junction*	
97.45		*Knighton Junction*	
98.02		*Knighton Tunnel (south portal)*	
98.07		*Knighton Tunnel (north portal)*	
99.07		**LEICESTER**	**32**
103.63		**Syston**	**34**
103.72		*Syston South Junction*	
104.25		*Syston North Junction*	
106.50		**Sileby**	**35**
108.00		*Mountsorrel*	
108.52		**Barrow-Upon-Soar**	**35**
111.22		*Loughborough South Junction*	
111.46		**LOUGHBOROUGH**	**36**
118.01		*Ratcliffe South Junction*	
118.66		*Redhill Tunnels (south portals)*	
118.73		*Redhill Tunnel fast line (north portal)*	
118.74		*Redhill Tunnel slow line (north portal)*	
119.17		*Trent South Junction*	
119.69		*Trent East Junction*	
121.26		*Toton Junction*	
121.64		*Toton Centre*	
125.09		*Trowell Junction*	
129.68		**Langley Mill**	**41**
132.76		*Codnor Park Junction*	
133.67		*Pye Bridge Junction*	
135.11		*Alfreton Tunnel (south portal)*	
135.50		*Alfreton Tunnel (north portal)*	
136.07		**ALFRETON & MANSFIELD PARKWAY**	**42**
137.16		*Tibshelf & Blackwell Branch Junction*	
142.10		*Clay Cross South Junction*	
144.15		**LMR/ER Boundary**	
146.20		**CHESTERFIELD**	**44**
146.62		*Tapton Junction*	
151.44		**DRONFIELD**	**45**
152.49		*Bradway Tunnel (south portal)*	
153.61		*Bradway Tunnel (north portal)*	
153.73		*Dore South Junction*	
154.52		*Dore Station Junction*	
158.01		*East Bank Tunnel (south portal)*	
158.05		*East Bank Tunnel (north portal)*	
158.40		**SHEFFIELD**	**46**
158.76		*Nunnery Main Line Junction*	
160.18		*Mill Race Junction*	
161.52		*Wincobank Station Junction*	

(M.Ch)	(M .Ch)	Location	Page
161.70		**Meadowhall**	**47**
163.43		*Holmes Junction*	
163.77	*162.00*	*Rotherham Masborough*	
164.21	162.24	*Masborough North Junction*	
166.60	164.63	*Aldwarke Junction*	
168.71	**166.74**	**Swinton**	**48**
171.20	**16.56**	**Bolton-On_Dearne**	**49**
172.26	**15.50**	**Goldthorpe**	**49**
172.59	15.17	*Goldthrope Colliery Branch Junction*	
173.12	**14.64**	**Thurnscoe**	**49**
176.47	**11.29**	**Moorthorpe**	**50**
176.52	11.24	*Moorthorpe Junction*	
177.24	165.74	*South Kirby Junction*	
180.45	**169.15**	**Fitzwilliam**	**51**
183.23	171.73	*Hare Park Junction*	
184.52	*49.40*	*Crofton West Junction*	
185.16	*48.76*	*Oakenshaw Junction*	
185.64	*48.28*	*Calder Bridge Junction*	
186.34	*48.33*	*Turners lane Junction*	
188.67	**185.11**	**Normanton**	**52**
189.56	186.00	*Altofts Junction*	
191.13	187.37	*Methley Junction*	
193.58	**190.02**	**Woodlesford**	**53**
196.18	192.42	*Stourton Junction*	
197.16	193.40	*Hunslet South Junction*	
197.66	194.10	*Hunslet Station Junction*	
198.76	195.20	*Engine Shed Junction*	
199.30	195.54	*Whitehall Junction*	

2. The Aire Valley

(M.Ch)	(M .Ch)	Location	Page
199.75	196.19	*Wortley Junction*	
205.56	202.00	*Apperley Junction*	
207.19	203.43	*Thackley Tunnels (south portal)*	
208.07	204.31	*Thackley Tunnels (north portal)*	
209.30	205.54	*Shipley East junction*	
209.48	**205.72**	**Shipley**	**57**
209.56	206.00	*Shipley West Junction*	
209.62	206.06	*Shipley Tunnel (south portal)*	
209.65	206.09	*Shipley Tunnel (north portal)*	
210.27	**206.51**	**Saltaire**	**58**
212.32	208.56	*Bingley Tunnel (south portal)*	
212.39	208.63	*Bingley Tunnel (north portal)*	
212.44	**208.68**	**Bingley**	**58**
213.21	**209.45**	**Crossflats**	**58**
215.62	**212.06**	**Keighley**	**59**
215.78	212.22	*Keighley Station Junction*	
218.60	**215.04**	**Steeton & Silsden**	**59**
221.76	**218.20**	**Cononley**	**60**
224.77	**221.21**	**Skipton**	**61**
225.11	221.35	*Skipton Middle Junction*	
228.55	**224.79**	**Gargrave**	**61**
234.76	**231.20**	**Hellifield**	**63**
236.17	**232.41**	**Long Preston**	**63**

(M.Ch)	(M .Ch)	Location	Page
3. The Settle & Carlisle			
238.18	234.42	*Settle Junction*	
240.16	**236.40**	**Settle**	**64**
242.30	238.54	*Stainforth tunnel (south portal)*	
242.35	238.59	*Stainforth tunnel (north portal)*	
246.19	**242.43**	**Horton In Ribblesdale**	**65**
250.76	**247.20**	**Ribblehead**	**66**
253.01	249.25	*Blea Moor Tunnel (south portal)*	
254.41	250.65	*Blea Moor Tunnel (north portal)*	
257.08	**253.32**	**Dent**	**67**
257.67	254.11	*Rise Hill Tunnel (south portal)*	
258.42	254.66	*Rise Hill Tunnel (north portal)*	
260.29	**256.53**	**Garsdale**	**68**
261.15	257.39	*Moorcock Tunnel (south portal)*	
261.20	257.44	*Moorcock Tunnel (north portal)*	
262.14	258.38	*Shotlock Hill Tunnel (south portal)*	
262.19	258.43	*Shotlock Hill Tunnel (north portal)*	
263.33	**259.57**	***AIS GILL SUMMIT (1,167ft.)***	**68**
267.79	264.23	*Birkett Tunnel (south portal)*	
268.18	264.42	*Birkett Tunnel (north portal)*	
270.23	266.47	**Kirkby Stephen**	**71**
272.56	269.00	*Crosby Garrett Tunnel (south portal)*	
272.64	269.08	*Crosby Garrett Tunnel (north portal)*	
276.69	273.13	*Helm Tunnel (south portal)*	
277.15	273.39	*Helm Tunnel (north portal)*	
280.78	**277.22**	**APPLEBY**	**73**
281.03	*277.27*	*Appleby North Junction*	
288.54	284.78	*Culgaith Tunnel (south portal)*	
289.04	285.28	*Culgaith Tunnel (north portal)*	
289.24	*285.48*	*Waste Bank Tunnel (south portal)*	
289.31	285.55	*Waste Bank Tunnel (north portal)*	
291.79	**288.23**	**Langwathby**	**75**
296.01	*292.25*	*Lazonby Tunnel (south portal)*	
296.06	*292.30*	*Lazonby Tunnel (north portal)*	
296.26	**292.50**	**Lazonby and Kirkoswald**	**76**
299.18	*295.42*	*Barton Wood Tunnel No. 1 (south portal)*	
299.27	*295.51*	*Barton Wood Tunnel No. 1 (north portal)*	
299.31	*295.55*	*Barton Wood Tunnel No. 2 (south portal)*	
299.43	*295.67*	*Barton Wood Tunnel No. 2 (north portal)*	
300.27	*296.51*	*Armathwaite Tunnel (south portal)*	
300.42	*296.66*	*Armathwaite Tunnel (north portal)*	
301.65	**298.09**	**Armathwaite**	**77**
310.68	307.12	*Petteril Bridge Junction*	
311.07	59.45	*London Road Junction*	
311.44	68.73	*Carlisle South Junction*	
311.60	**69.09/0.00**	**CARLISLE**	**79**

(M.Ch)	(M .Ch)	Location	Page
4. The West Coast Main Line			
313.59	1.79	*Kingmoor*	
319.07	7.27	*Admiralty Junction Sidings*	
319.44	7.64	*Mossband Junction*	
319.60	**8.00**	**LMR/ScR Boundary**	
320.37	8.57	*Gretna Junction*	
5. The Glasgow & South Western Railway			
321.38	**115.12**	**Gretna Green**	**99**
326.55	109.75	*Eastriggs*	
329.38	**107.12**	**Annan**	**101**
344.04	92.46	*Dumfries South Junction*	
344.67	**91.63**	**DUMFRIES**	**105**
345.02	91.48	*Maxwelltown Goods junction*	
362.61	73.69	*Drumlanrig Tunnel (south portal)*	
363.45	73.05	*Drumlanrig Tunnel (north portal)*	
370.75	**65.55**	**Sanquhar**	**110**
374.19	**62.31**	**Kirkconnel**	**110**
381.50	**55.00**	**New Cumnock**	**113**
382.45	54.05	*Bank Junction*	
384.14	**52.36**	***Polquhap Summit***	
389.04	**47.46**	**Auchinleck**	**114**
393.48	43.02	*Mauchline Junction*	
394.79	41.51	*Mossgiel Tunnel (south portal)*	
395.30	41.20	*Mossgiel Tunnel (north portal)*	
400.80	35.50	*Hurlford*	
402.09	34.41	*Kay Park Junction*	
402.71	**33.59**	**KILMARNOCK**	**117**
403.02	33.48	*Kilmarnock Junction*	
405.02	**21.48**	**Kilmaurs**	**118**
408.30	**18.20**	**Stewarton**	**118**
410.48	**16.02**	**Dunlop**	**119**
419.53	**6.77**	**Barrhead**	**120**
421.20	**5.30**	**Nitshill**	**121**
421.74	**4.56**	**Priesthill & Darnley**	**121**
422.60	**3.70**	**Kennishead**	**121**
423.48	3.02	*Busby Junction*	
423.70	**2.60**	**Pollokshaws West**	**121**
424.70	**1.60**	**Crossmyloof**	**122**
425.31	1.19/0.00	*Muirhouse South Junction*	
425.46	0.15	*Muirhouse Central Junction (1)*	
425.50	0.19	*Muirhouse Central Junction (2)*	
425.63	0.32	*Muirhouse North Junction*	
426.21	101.39	*Eglington Street Junction*	
426.38	101.56	*Bridge Street Junction*	
427.08	**102.26**	**GLASGOW CENTRAL**	**122**